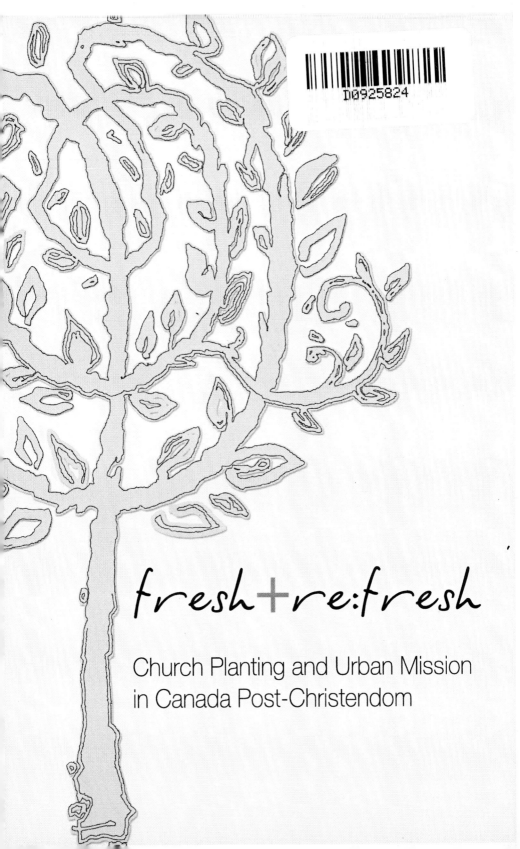

fresh+re:fresh

Church Planting and Urban Mission
in Canada Post-Christendom

Fresh+re:fresh: Church Planting and Urban Mission in Canada Post-Christendom

Published in Eagle, Idaho, by Allelon Publishing
PO Box 639
Eagle, ID 83616
www.allelonpublishing.org

First edition 2009
Cover design: David Vierzbicki

ISBN 10: 0-9777184-2-5
ISBN 13: 978-0-9777184-2-9
Printed in the United Sates of America
13 12 11 10 09 08 07 06   1 2 3 4 5 6 7 8 9

Church Planting and Urban Mission in Canada Post-Christendom

Fresh+re:fresh

Edited by: Leonard Hjalmarson and Brent Toderash

ALLELON
MISSIONAL SERIES
MISSION IN WESTERN CULTURE PROJECT

Contents

Fresh+re:fresh

Church Planting and Urban Mission in Canada Post-Christendom

Brent Toderash and Len Hjalmarson

Len is a writer, pastor, and software developer living among the orchards and vineyards of Kelowna, B.C. He is a regional representative for RESONATE and writes at Missional Journey, and NextReformation.com. He was a contributor and editor of *Voices of the Virtual World* (Volume One of The Wikiklesia Project). Len is finishing a DMin in Leadership and Spirituality at ACTS Seminary in Langley, B.C. Len is the father of two young ladies, is harried by a Siamese cat, and is married to Betty, a registered nurse who works with women in transition. Len blogs at www.nextreformation.com and www.allelon.org.

Brent is a thinker and writer living in Winnipeg, Manitoba. He was a contributor to the award winning Wikiklesia Project. Brent has been an entrepreneur, part-owner of an ISP, a technology and marketing consultant, and publisher of a Linux advocacy website. Currently he is a freelance writer, attempting to live his life and share his faith as best he can.

Fresh+re:fresh – A Foreword

- Len Hjalmarson

"Then, suddenly, out of the strange silence and strange motion
there came a tremendous roar.
The Eagle Rock on the south wall, about a half a mile up the valley,
gave way and I saw it falling in thousands of…great boulders.

"As soon as those rock avalanches fell,
the streams began to sing new songs…by what at first sight
seemed pure confounded confusion and ruin,
the landscapes were enriched."

John Muir, *The Earthquake*

We live in a time of tremendous shaking. Recent surveys by the Barna group[1] and others indicate that more and more believers do not attend an established church on a regular basis. Yet at the same time, there is a growing spiritual hunger: a hunger for transcendence, a hunger for significant relationships, and a hunger to connect with meaning. Reggie McNeal says of so-called "secular" culture that it is now "more spiritual than the church culture."[2]

---

[1] George Barna, *Revolution* (Carol Stream: Tyndale House, 2005) See also the Pew Survey.

[2] He writes that, "The first Reformation was about freeing the church. The new Reformation is about freeing God's people from the church (the institution). The original Reformation decentralized the church. The new Reformation decentralizes ministry. The former Reformation occurred when clergy were no longer willing to take marching orders from the Pope. The current Reformation finds church members no longer willing for clergy to script their personal spiritual ministry journey. The last

2

There have been other such times in history, when cultural shift left the Church on shaky ground because it was wedded to a world that was passing away. The Reformation, standing in the early days of the Enlightenment, was such a time. Likewise the Old Testament documents similar transitions, explored by scholars like Walter Brueggemann.

In *Cadences of Home*[3] Brueggemann documents the first *diaspora* when the Israelites became exiles, living far from Jerusalem in Babylon. He describes this theologically as the movement "from Temple to text," and argues that while there was a loss of political freedom, this was a time of tremendous theological creativity: of a rediscovery of the freedom of God and a reappropriation of faith and hope. Could it be that when everything is shaken we are invited to a new level of dependence and a renewed faith?

Other scholars from other disciplines are asking that question. In *The Upside of Down*, for example, Thomas Homer-Dixon writes, "We can get ready in advance to turn to our advantage any breakdown that does occur. We can boost the chances that it will lead to renewal by being well prepared, nimble and smart and by learning to recognize its many warning signs."[4] Elsewhere he coins a word for the process of renewal that comes through breakdown: *catagenesis*. *Catagenesis* describes a process that results when complex adaptive systems adapt to new conditions.

When we began to imagine this project we gathered practitioners who are exploring new territory, often in old ways. The contributors are all confident that the Church will survive into the future in some form, and are not allied to structures but rather to Jesus. Wineskins will change; the Spirit who indwells the Body is the unchanging Lord.

Reformation moved the church closer to home. The new Reformation is moving the church closer to the world. *The Present Future* (San Francisco: Jossey-Bass, 2003).

[3] Walter Brueggemann, *Cadences of Home* (Louisville: Westminster John-Knox Press, 1997).

[4] Thomas Homer-Dixon, *The Upside of Down: Catastrophe, Creativity, and the Renewal of Civilization* (Vintage Canada: Toronto, 2007) 2021.

At the same time, we are rooted in our culture. We sense the challenge of transition, the threat to our own equilibrium, and more deeply, to our sense of identity as leaders. We are accustomed to managing problems and comforting people. Suddenly the problems are so unique that we have no ready answers. That isn't easy to admit. Moreover, at some level we fear the unknown and the pain of transition. The legacy of Constantine and of the Enlightenment gave us a Church of the centre, a Church allied with the dominant forms of economic, intellectual, cultural and social life. We have been wealthy and comfortable, and sometimes we thought, "in need of nothing." The current shaking exposes our insecurity, our need for comfort, and at times, our compromises.

During the span of Christendom,[5] the Church knew both success and power. In our recent history we adopted Industrial Age models of leadership, and rational measures of success.[6] By those measures we were doing fairly well.[7] We have been less aware of how these emphases shaped us and our ministry in turn and how our gospel came to mirror "worldly wisdom," drained of spiritual life and power.

For this reason, we must be thankful. The present shaking has helped us to "see our seeing." We are becoming aware of the dominant texts of our culture and their impact on our theology and practice. We have been forced to ask new questions and to strip away layers of assumptions about the gospel and culture and the relationship between the two. When old maps no longer describe the territory, we begin to rely on an inner

---

[5] I use "Christendom" to represent the settled context of religious life in cooperation with the state, a cultural compromise, as opposed to Christianity, which I take to be the movement that Jesus initiated. Under Constantine, Christianity moved from a subversive, marginalized and persecuted movement to "a religious institution with its attendant structures, priesthood and sacraments." For more on this see Stuart Murray, *Post-Christendom: Church and Mission in a Strange New World.* (London: Authentic Media, 2004) or Guder, Ed. *Missional Church.* (Grand Rapids, MI: Wm. B. Eerdmans, 1998) 190-195.

[6] The ABCs – attendance, buildings and cash. I suggest we find a new set of ABCs: authenticity, belonging, and cultivating Christ.

[7] Skye Jethani, the managing editor of Leadership Magazine, recently penned a tongue-in-cheek article for the online Out of Ur blog titled, "Great is Thy Effectiveness." (August 12, 2008) http://blog.christianitytoday.com/outofur.

vision. When our natural sight is dim, we remember faith and that those before us also "went out, not knowing where they were going." We learn new songs. In our need we are opening new spaces for conversation and for conversion. In effect, we are rediscovering interdependence and a larger interpretive community.

Taxonomy: Inherited versus Emerging

In this volume, we explore the Canadian cultural landscape and the intersection of faith and culture through the lenses of three groups of practitioners. It's helpful to begin that exploration with a taxonomy. Stuart Murray in *Church After Christendom* distinguishes between "inherited" and "emerging" churches,[8] a more helpful framework than emerging vs. institutional. Murray notes that all church is "inherited" to some degree, then suggests three types of emergence, some of which are closer than others to *inheritance*.

> * churches emerging **from** inherited church through processes of renewal and transformation. The outcome is not another church, but a church more or less radically different from the past in structure, ethos, style, focus or activity.

> * churches emerging **out of** inherited church through processes of community engagement, liturgical exploration, church planting or missional reflection. The outcome is a new, or embryonic church, that becomes more or less autonomous.

> * churches emerging **within** a particular context without the shaping influence of or significant connection to inherited church. The outcome is a new church, which may be more or less radical, that will need to build links with other churches.

Murray calls for open conversations between various groups rather than formal consultation. We need to hear the stories as we attempt to reengage our culture, thus becoming a learning community.[9] He offers

---

[8] Stuart Murray, *Church After Christendom* (Waynesboro, GA: Paternoster Press, 2004) 113.

[9] http://en.wikipedia.org/wiki/Learning_community

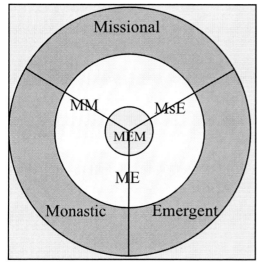

Missional	Monastic	Emergent
Missio Dei	Vows	Margins
Gpl of Kingdom	Place	Subversive/ Alternative
Academy	Poor	Place
Leadership	Prayer	Participatory
/enant Community		The Arts/ Mystery

Peter with the Jerusalem church in Acts 11 as a paradigm for conversation.[10] The church planters, mentors and urban missionaries who tell their stories in these pages are all *ekklesial* workers, in relation at some level to the larger story of which they are a local and temporal expression.

But there are other stories of engagement told here. You will also hear the stories of workers who are in more traditional settings, and who inherited leadership in an existing faith community and who are on a journey of renewal and missional engagement.

The third group represented here are mentors of church planters and urban missionaries. Their perspective is unique because they stand in the midst of cultural change, having been raised in one world but having set foot on a new shore. Their excitement at this adventure is often palpable. By nature they are learners, and by their own admission, they are discovering new questions as they walk alongside others in the new world. Reggie McNeal writes:

> Culture roils and churns in the collision of the old with the new. At the dawn of the third Christian millennium, continuity battles with discontinuity; the emergent dances with what is passing away. Leaders of spiritual enterprises, like many of the adherents

---

[10] Murray describes the key elements as storytelling, theological reflection, critical questioning, careful listening, passionate advocacy and thoughtful conclusion (115).

of the faith, have oars in both currents. The challenge involves getting as many through the rapids as possible, knowing some will never make it. The success of the mission largely depends on the ability of the leader, the river guide, to know how to "read" the water.[11]

Any medical student knows that treatment is dependent on accurate diagnosis. A plethora of books, articles and dissertations are attempting to help us exegete our culture.[12] At the same time, a variety of fresh expressions are under the spotlight, and books and papers are rising from observers.[13] One of the recent taxonomies proposed by Tom Sine and others is the observation of at least four distinct streams of renewal in the missional, monastic, mosaic and emergent movements.[14] If Thomas Homer-Dixon is right that synergistic energy can result in *catagenesis* in complex systems, we may be observing the emergence of conditions that will engender a new storm system for change.

We asked some specific questions of the church planters and urban missionaries who offered to tell their stories. For example, we asked them to reflect on the following:

* What is your theological grid for the gospel and culture?
* What is your view of leadership, and how has your understanding changed as "the rubber hits the road?"
* What is your understanding of spiritual formation, and how does

---

[11] Reggie McNeal, *A Work of Heart* (San Franciso: Jossey-Bass, 2000) 79.

[12] For example, James K.A. Smith, *Who's Afraid of Postmodernism*? and *Everyday Theology*, Kevin Vanhoozer, Ed. and Duane K. Friesen, *Artists, Citizens and Philosophers: Seeking the Peace of the City*, Vinoth Ramachandra, *Subverting Global Myths* and at ALLELON Alan Roxburgh's *Missional Mapmaking* series. On the secular side, Thomas Homer-Dixon, *The Up Side of Down* and Naomi Klein, *Shock Doctrine*.

[13] For example, *Mission-Shaped Church* is a report from a working group within the Church of England (2003) and Eddie Gibbs and Ryan Bolger published *Emerging Churches* in 2005.

[14] Tom Sine, *The New Conspirators* (Downer's Grove: IVP, 2008). I have recently blogged about the creative potential growing out of the convergence of these streams and the diagram here comes from those reflections. http://nextreformation.com/?p=2222.

it relate to missional engagement?

* How does your understanding of *ekklesia* relate to the kingdom of God?
* What new questions are forming as you engage in community building and mission?
* Have you embraced specific spiritual practices?
* Who are your mentors or models (dead or alive)?

As we recognize the complexity of missional re-engagement with our culture we are moving beyond pragmatism. Church planters and those attempting to bring renewal to established churches are asking new questions about the nature of God and his mission. There is a renewed interest in theology and Christology, and a re-engagement with Trinitarian foundations. Moreover, there is a re-engagement with memory and the stories that anchor Christian identity.

Memory and Subversion

In Scripture we are constantly reminded of our connection to the land, and of our identity as a *covenant people.* In times of exile, distant from home, we face the unique danger of loss of memory and loss of roots. In that void, we are apt to believe the promises of the Empire to give us a home, to bring us security, to provide meaning and to offer unlimited consumption in an eternal Now. Who needs memory when life is so good today? Who needs the interdependence of community when we have everything we need?[15] How do we sing the Lord's song in a foreign land? Walter Brueggemann reminds us that:

> Only through the practice of memory will new possibility emerge. Without some form of memory, this sentence you are reading would make no sense...Without memory we become imprisoned in an absolute present, unaware of the direction we have come from, and therefore what direction we are heading in. Without

---

[15]One of the current buzzwords appearing on church billboards is "community." I am reminded of John Driver's comment. "By nature the church is a community and experiences communion. The question before the people of God is: What kind of community will we be?" (*Community and Commitment.* Scottdale: Herald Press, 1976) 28.

memory there can be no momentum, no discernible passage of time, and therefore no movement or velocity...[16]

All these things come together in the New Testament at the Lord's Table. The story of Passover is brought into the present, and the memories of deliverance and the hope for a just future become one story. "This is the new covenant in my blood. Do this in memory of Me." Again Brueggemann writes:

> Precisely because of being broken and poured out, this bread and wine will never be fully accommodated to the interests of the old age. The world wants the bread unbroken and the wine still filling the cup. The world yearns for unrisking gods and transformed humanity. But in our eating and drinking at this table we know better. We will not have these subversive alternatives rendered void.[17]

So subversion becomes a dominant theme as we consider the future of the Jesus movement in Canada. Brian McLaren, in *Everything Must Change,* writes that "the gods of progress — with names like Higher Consumption, More Growth and Rising Productivity — inspire a hymn, called not "Holy, holy, holy," but "Faster, Faster, Faster."[18] It's difficult to imagine a new and better world when we are moving at a speed that doesn't allow time for reflection. Moreover, if we are satiated, we have no need to hope for a better world. We are content with the eternal *Now*. Truly, the Empire offers good news and the only gospel we need is a spiritual one divorced from this world.[19]

Or is it? If we open our eyes we can see the writing on the wall as the speed and intensity of our consumptive lifestyle catches up with us. We

---

[16]Walter Brueggemann, *Hopeful Imagination* (Minneapolis: Augsburg Fortress Press, 2004), 56.

[17] Walter Brueggemann, "Covenant as a Subversive Paradigm." This article appeared in the *Christian Century*, November 12, 1980, pp. 1094-1099.

[18] Brian McLaren, *Everything Must Change* (Thomas Nelson, 2007) 193.

[19] In this connection see the recent work of N.T. Wright, *Surprised by Hope: Rethinking Heaven, the Resurrection and the Mission of the Church* (New York: HarperCollins, 2008).

are reaching the limits of our environment to support us, and we are beyond the bounds of equity. Popular religion has become a religion of immanence, because the risk of a transcendent God is the risk of judgment. We tamed God because only then could we avoid the call to justice. We embraced distraction because only then could we avoid the still, small voice that calls us to remember who we are.

> Driven hard and fast, we lack the time to allow alternate worlds and possibilities to form, careening past small turnings and exits, bound to follow the obvious straight paths of the present arrangement. Yet if we stop and wait, and close our eyes to the "buy now, take me now" images, we will begin to remember, new worlds will form and new exits will become apparent. Before change, comes waiting.[20]

Few of us have a love of waiting. Neither do we readily embrace these liminal spaces. We cry out like Bono:

> *Yahweh, Yahweh*
> *Always pain before a child is born*
> *Yahweh, Yahweh*
> *Why the dark before the dawn?*[21]

Re-Entering Our Neighbourhoods

We worship the child born in Bethlehem. God showed up in Israel in a way no one expected. He simply did not fit the categories. He arrived to ordinary people in an obscure place. Those who should have seen clearly saw nothing, while those who were said to be blind saw clearly.

Canadian church planters *see*. They have their eyes open. They are preparing for God's surprising newness. The disciplines of readiness are prayer, study, the Table, hospitality and worship, the pursuit of justice, and all these pursued in community. Together we listen, we pray, and we

---

[20] Brueggemann, Op Cit. 57.

[21] U2, "Yahweh." From *How to Dismantle an Atomic Bomb*, 2004. See also the song newly released by Brian McLaren in collaboration with *The Restoration Project*, "11:57."

look for opportunities to enter the ordinary stories of ordinary people in obscure places. It is to the lowly and meek that Jesus comes.

Canadian church planters are *humble.* They re-enter their neighbourhoods, not with a sense of their own importance, as if their efforts will bring in the kingdom, but rather in the humility of knowing that all their work is merely a mustard seed for the future. We are "prophets of a future not our own" (Romero).

Canadian church planters are *vulnerable.* For many years we have extracted people from their neighbourhoods and from the host culture and kept them busy with meetings and programs. Re-entering our neighbourhoods and meeting people where they live feels strange and vulnerable. Yet "the word became flesh and dwelt among us." In Jesus God became weak and vulnerable. We are sent as Jesus was sent.

Recently a Canadian seminary professor remarked to me that he has lived all his life in Canada, but he still could not identify a Canadian consensus around the meaning of community. I like Henri Nouwen's suggestion, and I think the good news is that *the Father invites us all to come home.*[22]

Canadian church planters are *visionary.* What would it mean to become a new community: a living temple of the loving Presence of God, a safe house for the sake of the world? Canadian church planters are re-imagining church for the new world. Metaphors and vision are being reborn as we shed modern strictures. Some metaphors relate more readily to the current transition we find ourselves in as we search for new wineskins to replace the ones that are crumbling.[23]

Somewhere Howard Snyder remarked that, *"It isn't the Church of God that has a mission in the world, it's the God of Mission who has a Church in the*

---

[22] Henri Nouwen, *Lifesigns* (New York: Doubleday, 1986).

[23] Walter Brueggemann remarks in *Cadences of Home* that the time of the exile was a particularly fertile time for theological work, a liminal place as the community moved from temple to text.

world.[24] God is breaking down our definitions and resetting the boundaries.

Canadian church planters *understand context*. The incarnation is much more than God entering human experience or some spiritual transaction divorced from this world; it is God revealed and encountered in place. Simon Carey Holt writes:

> The Christian faith is one of God's interaction with the physical world. From the stories of Creation and Incarnation to the transforming presence of the Spirit in all the earth, it's hard to fathom a Christian theology that does not treat the neighborhood as significant. God is revealed and encountered in place...Our call to mission is a call to discern, embody and proclaim the presence of God where we are. It's a call to neighborhood.[25]

Becoming missional has to do with where the boundary markers are being placed as we define the church. What is in-bounds? What is out-of-bounds? The boundary markers for the church should be determined by where the gifts and callings of God's people take them.[26] Or as one friend put it, "the work of the church is wherever God's people are situated."

Frost and Hirsch share a story that captures the shift. A visitor to an Australian outback cattle ranch was intrigued by the seemingly endless miles of farming country with no sign of any fences. He asked a local

---

[24] Howard Snyder, source unknown.

[25] Simon Carey Holt, *God Next Door: Spirituality and Mission in the Neighborhood* (Melbourne: Acorn Press, 2006) 63. Elsewhere he notes Martin Heidegger's assertion that to be human is to dwell. "Man *is* only in so far as he dwells." By dwelling, Heidegger means more than simply residing. Any living creature can reside. But to be human is to inhabit a place—to experience it from the inside—and allow that place to inhabit us. In a sense, it's this inhabiting that turns a neutral, empty space into a fully human place invested with meaning." 60.

[26] See Stuart Murray's discussion in *Church After Christendom* (pp.26ff) as well as Jim Petersen, *Church Without Walls* (Colorado Springs: NAVPRESS, 1992).

rancher how he kept track of his cattle. The rancher replied, "Oh that's no problem. Out here we dig wells instead of building fences."[27]

If believers are to seize the opportunities God brings their way in the neighbourhood and across society, and if they could proceed confident of support from others in the body, church must be redefined. Instead of church as somewhere we go, church is where we live. Instead of extracting believers from their daily lives, we imagine them as missionaries in their communities, permeating society like salt and light.

If we organize ourselves around mission rather than around church, we will have to find new measures of success.[28] When we enter our neighbourhoods in small and ordinary ways, we lose the drama of theatre that plays out at carefully orchestrated meetings on Sunday mornings. Life becomes ordinary and simpler. When our dominant forms are more organic, we will find new ways to gauge growth. God was veiled in flesh in Jesus. The hiddenness of the incarnation, God at table with us, walking among us, calls us to a missional paradigm. Mission is our apostolic inheritance, a faithful response to God's grace.

Cultural Distance and New Metaphors

In his article here David Fitch will tell us that in the old days of church planting twenty years ago we didn't have to cross significant cultural barriers to make a convert. Mega-churches could be grown in large cities relatively quickly, because people knew the Christian stories. They might have attended Sunday school or Christian camp. Even if they had never crossed the threshold of a church, they may have been raised in Christian

---

[27] Alan Hirsch and Michael Frost, *The Shaping of Things to Come* (Peabody: Hendrickson Publishers, 2003).

[28] A recent article by Brad Sargent, "Assessing Ministry in Emerging Cultures" offers not another assessment inventory, but an argument that using old tools results in zero validity. He writes that, "One of the major problems with applying existing assessment tools to situations in emerging cultures is that the tools' underlying cultural, theological, and philosophical presuppositions generally don't match with those of the cultures they claim to "measure"...it's a test for apples being used on oranges..." Online http://futuristguy.wordpress.com.

homes or heard the gospel on TV or radio. Increasingly this is not the case.

The cultural distance scale was devised by Ralph Winter[29] to demonstrate the gap between those who know the Christian story on one hand, and those who do not on the other. In short, we set ourselves and others on a scale from m0 on the left to m4 on the right in order to "see" the gap we must cross in order to authentically proclaim the gospel.

Each movement along the scale from left to right indicates a barrier one must cross to bring the gospel. The common example is language, a step from m0 to m1. The step from m1 to m2 would be from a "Christian" context to a context where there is popular awareness (perhaps having heard bad things about the church), or previous rejection. From m2 to m3 there is no real knowledge of Christianity at all: this is an alternative culture or ethnic group. From m3 to m4 is the greatest distance and often includes active resistance.

The Edict of Milan and Constantine's bargain with the church provided a uniform context in the western world for 1600 years. The church has largely conformed to that mode and is comfortable working with the m0 to m1 regions. Now, however, that region is vanishing and we are forced to move beyond those simple barriers to m2 and even m3, all in our own neighbourhoods. In Christendom "outreach" often worked. In post-Christendom and the pluralistic environment, the cultural distance has increased and our local context has become missional.

Ralph Winter uses the terms modality and sodality to talk about two different manifestations of the church.[30] Modality is more generalized, sodality more specialized. They are like the two phases of water: liquid and solid. Solid is more reliable, liquid is more dynamic and flexible. But both are water; both represent a truth about the church.

---

[29] Ralph Winter and Bruce Koch, Finishing the Task: The Unreached People's Challenge," in *Perspectives on the World Christian Movement*, 3rd ed., ed. Ralph D. Winter and Steven C. Hawthorne (Carlisle: Paternoster Press, 1999) 509-524.
[30] Ralph D. Winter, "The Two Structures of God's Redemptive Mission," Address to the All Asia Mission Consultation in Seoul, Korea, 1973.

In these transitional times sodality is becoming more critical. Sodality may lack obvious structure and have a short life, like the mushroom. The thin and spidery web that supports this type of fungus grows and spreads underground and can exist for tens of yards, without any surface manifestation. It appears suddenly: you walk in the evening and you see only green grass. The next morning you spy three mushrooms, which exist for a day or two, then disappear as suddenly and mysteriously.

The mushroom disappears, yet the hidden network remains, and may even be growing and expanding.[31]

The disappearance of the mushroom does not mean the network is unhealthy. The short life of a "mushroom" church doesn't mean it was not significant in the economy of the kingdom. Sometimes we attempt to preserve what we should let die. In an interview at Next-Wave, Neil Cole comments:

> The numbers of people can be deceptive. You can have many people and not be fruitful. You might just be putting on a better show than the guy around the corner. What we are looking for is fruitfulness.
>
> For instance we don't care if our churches live a year, twenty years, or a hundred years. We care that while they live, they give birth. We may start a church that lasts a year, but while it lives, it births two daughter churches. That is a success. We think that if every church reproduces in that way, then the Kingdom of God will continue and grow.
>
> But if we think that every church has to last forever, we will try to do everything we can to keep it alive artificially, and that's not

---

[31] The rhizome as a metaphor for underground organic networks relating to growth was first examined by Deleuze. Karl Raschke examines the concept carefully in his latest book, *GloboChrist: The Great Commission Takes a Postmodern Turn.* (Grand Rapids: Baker Book House, 2008).

good. We find fruitfulness most often in the small, not the large. Growing larger does not seem to be the key.[32]

Success is often defined by things we can measure: the ABC's (attendance, buildings, cash).[33] How do we measure transformation? How do we measure belonging? Networks are about belonging. Joel Myers writes that stories are the measuring tools of belonging.[34] Too much of our desire for assessment is related to the need for control. Rosemary Neave writes that, "This is where networks as a structure come into their own. They reflect a commitment to connect rather than to control; to share information rather than to ration it; to disperse power rather than gather it into the centre…[35]

Monasticism, Missional Orders and Leadership Lenses

One of the drawbacks of our long focus on leadership is that we have neglected environmental factors: leaders always exist in a particular soil as a particular culture. The community is the more foundational reality, and that is part of what Paul was trying to express with his "body" language. Paul talks and theologizes a great deal about the body – not that much about leaders.

In the end, a few leaders aren't going to change the world. But what possibilities might there be in a whole army on fire for Christ? Finally Jesus is less interested in shaping a few leaders than in transforming the world, and a transformed world begins with the work of God in the church. Gerhard Lohfink writes:

---

[32] "Growing God's Kingdom from the Harvest" Interview with Neil Cole at Next Wave online, November, 2005.

[33] In chapter one of *The Great Giveaway* David Fitch writes that, "Our focus on numbers, bigness and large institutions is rooted in two of America's sacred cows: the autonomy of the individual and the necessity to organize for economic efficiency." (Grand Rapids, MI: Baker Books, 2005) 33.

[34] Joel Myers, *The Search to Belong* (Grand Rapids: Zondervan, 2003) 69.

[35] Rosemary Neave, "Reimagining the Church." Study Leave Report, Nov. 2006.

There must be a place – visible, tangible – where the salvation of the world may begin: that is, where the world becomes what it is supposed to be according to God's plan. Beginning at that place, the new thing can spread abroad. All must have the chance to behold and test this new thing. Then, if they want to, they can allow themselves to be drawn into the story of salvation God is creating. Only in that way is freedom preserved.[36]

There have been two approaches to monastic orders in history: the western approach, and the eastern. The differences are significant, and it is from the western monastics that we find a legacy for our time. George C. Hunter III writes:

> ...the Eastern monasteries organized to protest and escape from the materialism of the Roman world and the corruption of the Church; the Celtic monasteries organized to penetrate the pagan world and to extend the Church. The eastern monks often withdrew from the world into monasteries to save and cultivate their own souls; Celtic leaders often organized monastic communities to save other people's souls. The leaders of the Eastern monasteries located their monasteries in isolated locations, off the beaten track; the Celtic Christians built their monastic communities in locations accessible to the traffic of the time, like proximity to settlements, or on hilltops, or on islands near the established sea lanes.[37]

Can new monastic communities and missional orders help us move beyond the leader/follower debate, and into missional effectiveness in our neighbourhoods?

If we can rediscover a rooted spirituality, embracing the local, embracing rhythms and relationships, then the answer is "yes." We will never greatly impact the world until we move beyond the things that distract us, and attract us. We are formed by the soil we grow in, and most of us

---

[36] Gerhard Lohfink, *Does God Need the Church: Toward a Theology of the People of God* (New York: Liturgical Press, 1996).

[37] George Hunter III, *The Celtic Way of Evangelism* (Abingdon Press, 1997).

grow primarily in the soil of a materialistic culture. This is our "community of virtue,"[38] and we receive most of our shaping messages from CNN, MTV, Hollywood and Madison Avenue. Culture is a cultivating force.

But if that is true, then our only hope for impacting the world is to form an alternative culture, with its own values and purpose. That is what Jesus' preaching was all about. He did not say, "I came that you might have church, and that more abundantly." Instead, he spoke of the kingdom of God. The goal is life, but not the life offered by the Disney Channel.

The big question of becoming like Jesus, then, is this: how do we become attentive to Jesus and participate with him in his work? We need counter-disciplines if we would be formed for the kingdom.[39] Disciplines that free us for the kingdom are traditional: worship and prayer, but also community, hospitality, generosity and mercy (or justice). These kinds of practices move the centre of our attention away from self and place it squarely on God and his kingdom.

Many years ago Jim Wallis wrote:

> The renewal of the church will come not through a recovery of personal experience or straight doctrine, nor through innovative projects of evangelism or social action, nor in creative techniques or liturgical worship, nor in the gift of tongues, nor in new budgets, new buildings, and new members. The renewal of the church will come about through the work of the Spirit in restoring and reconstituting the church as a local community whose common life bears the marks of radical obedience to the lordship of Jesus Christ.[40]

---

[38] William Cavanaugh, *Being Consumed: Economics and Christian Desire* (Grand Rapids: Wm B. Eerdmans, 2008) 9.

[39] See James K.A. Smith incisive discussion in *Who's Afraid of Postmodernism?* (Grand Rapids: Baker Academic, 2006) 104ff.

[40] Jim Wallis, *Agenda for Biblical People* (New York: Harper and Row, 1976) 101.

There are creative attempts to form kingdom culture all over North America. At *Life on the Vine* in Chicago the community is forming a missional order. Similarly, ALLELON is involved in forming a missional order. These conversations arise at the convergence zone of the missional movement and the new monasticism.[41] Growing numbers of people are aware that change will not come through better techniques or better programs. Something more basic is required. How will we be shaped into communities formed by the Spirit?

Other questions abound: How will our own lives be transformed so that in turn we can impact our neighbours? How do we partner with God in his movement into our neighbourhoods (Luke 10)? Where evangelism tends to aim at an individual decision that leaves self at the centre, and often extracts the convert from her context, mission is formed by a kingdom agenda that is interested in transformation rooted in daily life in our communities. While some worry that this is a renewal of legalism, it is truly a call to freedom. Henri Nouwen writes:

> A Rule offers "creative boundaries within which God's loving presence can be recognized and celebrated." It does not prescribe but invite, it does not force but guide, it does not threaten but warn, it does not instill fear but points to love. In this it is a call to freedom, freedom to love.[42]

Alan Roxburgh, of ALLELON Canada notes that "The vast majority of church leaders have no daily form of Christian practice or formation in their own lives." Moreover, which practices should one select? We have a wide variety of historic practices or disciplines to choose from. Too many choices generate anxiety and paralysis. Perhaps it matters less *what* we choose but *that* we choose. We have to find ground to stand on, and that ground must be in some sense communal. Roxburgh writes:

---

[41] See in particular, *Inhabiting the Church: Biblical Wisdom for a New Monasticism* (Eugene, OR: Wipf and Stock, 2008) and *The New Friars* (Downer's Grove: IVP, 2006), and *The Irresistible Revolution: Living as an Ordinary Radical* (Grand Rapids, MI: Zondervan, 2006).

[42] The Northumbria Community Online.

Just when formation in Christian practices is being recognized as an essential element for missional formation in local churches, a majority of local leaders have little sense of how to do this for themselves let alone lead their people in this way. And yet there is a hunger among leaders to discover again the ancient ways of formation. Conversations with leaders of the Northumbria Community more than a year ago revealed that increasing numbers of church leaders across the UK are entering into this ancient, well practiced way of the church. These practices of Christian life cross the boundaries of organized and 'organic' notions of church. The formation of an order provides the opportunity for many of us to move past the ideological divides so characteristic of recent conversations about the church and risk learning together about the way of formation for the sake of the church. It is this desire to invite leaders of all kinds to experiment together around a simple rule of life that lies at the basis of our desire to call leaders together to look at the form of such an order.

Finally, our models and lenses for leadership itself must be expanded. The models and lenses which were adopted and adapted during the Industrial Age no longer "work" or make sense in the post-Industrial Age, and our current lenses limit our sight.[43] In the last generation of evangelical churches, leadership has been characterized by *sola pastora* models. The pastor/teacher has been the key leadership gift, and anything like Biblical eldership and plurality has generally disappeared. However, there are signs of change and renewal.

Apostolic teams are being recovered. The language to describe these teams and their functioning varies according to received tradition and present context. But the roles that are appearing have familiar traits, with one exception. In *The Sky is Falling*, Alan Roxburgh describes *the poet*.

The poet helps people make sense of their experiences. The word in the prologue of John tells how Jesus "became flesh and lived among us." In a similar way, the poet shapes words so that what was hidden and

---

[43] See Kevin Vanhoozer's discussion of maps in *Christianity and the Postmodern Turn* (Grand Rapids, MI: Baker Book House, 2005) 86-87.

invisible becomes known. Poets remove the veil and give language to what people are experiencing. This is only possible when the poet him/herself lives within the traditions and narratives of the people – "living reflexively in the traditions...The poet listens to the rhythms and meanings occurring beneath the surface." [44]

But the poet also has a prophetic bent: "poets immerse themselves in the multiple stories running beneath the surface of the culture...feel the power of these stories and critique their claims and pretensions on the basis of the memory and tradition of the community."

The leadership of poets, however, is not expressed in a modern manner. Poets "are not so much advice-givers as image and metaphor framers... What churches need are not more entrepreneurial leaders with wonderful plans for their congregation's life, but poets with the imagination and gifting to cultivate environments within which people might again understand how their traditional narratives apply to them today...Many of the programs on church health can only lead the churches down more of the same utilitarian and technological dead ends that have contributed to the current malaise."

Finally, "poets make available a future that does not exist as yet; they are *eschatologically* oriented. From this environment, a missional imagination emerges." [45]

As we would expect, poets had little value in the churches of modernity. In modernity we sought to define problems toward a solution. But poets don't bring solutions; rather they bring questions that invite dialogue. Poets do not accept the view of a congregation as a tool for impacting the world, but as the location of God's work of redemption and the incipient present-future of the kingdom.

I am reminded of Eugene Peterson's call to rediscover leadership as a spiritual vocation. In *The Contemplative Pastor*, he writes:

---

[44] Alan Roxburgh, *The Sky is Falling: Leaders Lost in Transition* (Eagle, ID: ACI Publications, 2005) 164-166. For an extended discussion visit http://nextreformation.com/?p=2257.

[45] Ibid. 166.

The secularized mind is terrorized by mysteries. Thus it makes lists, labels people, assigns roles, and solves problems. But a solved life is a reduced life. These tightly buttoned-up people never take great faith risks or make convincing love talk. They deny or ignore the mysteries and diminish human existence to what can be managed, controlled, and fixed. We live in a cult of experts who explain and solve. The vast technological apparatus around us gives the impression that there is a tool for everything if we can only afford it. Pastors cast in the role of spiritual technologists are hard put to keep that role from absorbing everything else, since there are so many things that need to be and can, in fact, be fixed.

But "there are things," wrote Marianne Moore, "that are important beyond all this fiddle." The old time guide of souls asserts the priority of the "beyond" over "this fiddle." Who is available for this kind of work other than pastors? A few poets, maybe; and children, always. But children are not good guides, and most of the poets have lost interest in God. That leaves pastors as guides through the mysteries.[46]

May we learn to surrender to mystery and accept the kingdom as a gift. May God make us poets.

---

[46] Eugene Peterson, *The Contemplative Pastor* (Grand Rapids, MI: Wm B. Eerdmans, 1989) 65.

David Fitch

David Fitch is the founding pastor of Life on the Vine Christian Community – an emerging / missional church of the Christian and Missionary Alliance in the Northwest Suburbs of Chicago. (www.lifeonthevine.org). He is also Lindner Professor of Evangelical Theology at Northern Seminary, Lombard IL. He grew up in Hamilton, Ontario and has spent much time in Canada listening and ministering to missional church pastors / leaders / friends / denominational leaders. He is the author of numerous articles on church, culture and theological ethics in various journals. He is the author of *The Great Giveaway: Reclaiming the Mission of the Church from American Business, Para-Church Organizations, Psychotherapy, Consumer Capitalism and Other Modern Maladies* (Baker Books, 2005). David blogs at www.reclaimingthemission.com and is a frequent contributor to the Leadership blog located on the *Christianity Today* webzine http://blog.christianitytoday.com/outofur.

Fifty Years of Church Planting: The Story as I See it

– David Fitch

Over the last three decades, I have watched church planting change dramatically in Canada and the Northern parts of the United States. Back in the sixties/seventies, we used to send fifteen or twenty people from one local church into another place several towns over that was "under-churched." We would hold worship services, teach Sunday school, have a children's ministry. We would set up shop. We would choose a pastor who "had all the tools" as they would say. He (most often a male) would be young, energetic and able to work like crazy. We would send out pubic announcements expecting many who were looking for a church to just show up. And if we did the basic services well, then we assumed the little gathering would grow into a self-sustaining church in three years. In many ways, these church plants resembled franchises.

Church planting worked like this because there were still large numbers of Christians to draw from for a congregation. We were in the great post-WW2 expansion in North America. New towns and subdivisions were springing up left and right. And just as each town needed a supermarket, a library and public schools, so also it needed a church. One could assume that out of the many thousands moving here into these new habitats, some would be Christians and need a church. So we planted churches like franchised local grocery stores. This was the era of Christendom.

In the eighties, the focus on church planting changed. Post WW2 expansion had slowed. More and more of the suburban boomers had not returned to the churches of their youth. The focus of church planting shifted to recapturing these now unchurched people for Christ. Now when we went to plant a church we needed to first conduct marketing surveys. We asked what we could do to make church more relevant and user friendly.

The surveys focused on finding out what unchurched people were looking for. What turns them off of church? How can we do church in a way that relates to these people? How can we make church relevant so that the "unchurched" would come to our services? What could make church more attractive? We focused on delivering the services with "excellence" and "efficiency" characteristic of the marketplace. In these ways we planted churches like Wal-Marts. The seeker service and church growth methods were invented. Hundreds of boomer generation people came who had left the church a decade before. Many hundreds of people in traditional churches left as well for "the new and improved" big box churches. Today, hundreds of mega-churches exist across North America as a testimony to the "success" of this approach to church planting.

Church planting like this worked because there were still huge numbers of unchurched people who had once learned of Christ in the earliest years of their upbringing. These unchurched had some familiarity with who Jesus was. Deep within their boomer psyches, Jesus still carried credibility, even authority, even if they did consider the church obsolete. We assumed therefore that if we could just make Jesus more relevant and attractive (as opposed to their former experiences of church) they would come.

If the Bible could be communicated in a way that was meaningful to people's everyday life and needs, these unchurched would surely listen. And they did come. People making "decisions for Christ" multiplied. Church planting like this, however, still depended upon what was left of the vestiges of North American Christendom. A majority of the conversions were former high church catechumens "coming back to Jesus."[47] They had never made a "personal" decision to follow the Jesus

---

[47] Ironically many denominations still categorize these "decisions" as "conversion growth." Meanwhile more and more youth are leaving evangelical low churches for the high church traditions (Colleen Carroll, 2004). I wonder if the high church

they had earlier been taught about (most often in catechetical rote fashion). In this way, the seeker church movement was built upon Christendom.

The days of Christendom are fading fast, and a following change in mindset of those who would plant churches. As the number of Christians without a church shrinks, as the number of unchurched who once were catechumens of Christianity grows extinct, I have witnessed first hand a new wave of church planters who think of church planting in completely different ways. They are not interested in competing for the leftovers of Christendom. They resist the notion that the church is in need of just one more innovation. They are interested in nothing less than becoming missionaries, to plant churches cross culturally, to cross cultural barriers to people who have no knowledge or language about Jesus.

From Setting Up Grocery (Big-Box) Stores To Cultivating Gardens

For those of us born before 1970, this change is truly stunning. The landscape of post-Christendom demands we think about church planting with a new eye for faithfulness, truth and integrity. Among the new missional leaders, church is the name we give to a way of life, not a set of services. We do not plant an organized set of services; we inhabit a neighbourhood as the living embodied presence of Christ. Missional leaders now root themselves in a piece of geography for the long term – becoming not only missional but also incarnational.

When we plant today, we survey the land for the poor and the desperate, not just physically but emotionally and spiritually as well. We seek to plant seeds of ministry, kernels of forgiveness, new plantings of the gospel among "the poor (of all kinds)" and then by the Spirit water and nurture them into the life of God in Christ. We gather on Sunday, but not for evangelistic reasons. We gather to be formed into a missional people and then sent out into the neighbourhoods to minister grace, peace, love and the gospel of forgiveness and salvation.

---

traditions count them as (re)conversions as the low church evangelicals once did when their youth converted to evangelicalism?

The biggest part of church, then, is what goes on outside gathering. If the old ways of planting a church were like setting up a grocery store, now it is more like seeding a garden, cultivating it, and watching God grow it amidst the challenges of the rocks, weeds and thorns (I owe this metaphor to my co-pastors at Life on the Vine). What do these leaders look like? How can we walk alongside them? After hanging with a hundred or so of these leaders over the past few years, I have observed that missional leaders will most often be the following kinds of people.

Five Observations Concerning Missional Leaders

They Will Be Survivors

Enduring missional leaders must learn how to survive financially and spiritually for the long term. They must be able to hold down a job that does not consume them, but that enables them to live simply for the long term. In Christendom, the denominations used to pay someone to go plant a church. This would usually be one person who was unusually gifted and (based upon the above premises) could get a self-sufficient church going in three years. This person was in essence paid to extend an organization, open up a franchise, and set up a version of church that mirrored the distinctives of the denomination.

In the new post-Christendom, this doesn't make sense. In my opinion it takes at least five years of "seeding a community" before one even begins to see an ethos of community and new life develop that can be a cultural carrier-transmitter of the gospel. As a result, the new missional community leaders must have patience, steady faithfulness and the ability to live simply. They must be able to get jobs and not see the ministry as a privileged full time vocation. They must have a mental image of how they are going to sustain their lives financially, relationally, spiritually and personally. This must take the shape of a sustainable rhythm. In my experience, these kinds of leaders are often found among the young and disenchanted evangelicals. I have learned they merely need a vision and a support network and they are willing to sacrifice in ways my generation never would.

They Will Be Communal Shepherds

I have found that missional leaders are most often shepherds of an overall ethos of a community. They are not starting and managing an organization. They may not even be good at organization. Instead they are cultivating a communal sense of mission identity among a gathering people "for this time and place." It used to be every church planter had to be an extravert entrepreneur, someone who looked good and had the perfect family. Single people need not apply. This person had to be a good salesman (woman) and had to have endless energy. He or she had to set a vision, direct a course, motivate and sell.

It's true that many of these qualities are helpful in starting new things. Yet I have seen, in this new era, that the missional leader is more often someone who can take time and be with people. He or she will listen to people, discern the needs, articulate where we are going, and knit the community together in a common struggle with gentleness, encouragement, and listening. We do not gather as we once did to hear a charismatic leader preach an entertaining piece of inspiration. We do not gather for a professional piece of programmed worship experience. In the new post-Christendom we are coming together to be formed and shaped, supported and edified for the Mission as a band of brothers and sisters. Yes, we do gather on Sundays to hear the Word, to be nourished at the Table, and respond to what God is calling us to -- but we do all this not as individuals but as a community, a community "sent out" into mission.

These kinds of leaders do not grow on trees; they must be mentored in character for the patience and faithfulness such shepherding requires. The type A person who is always selling or programming something has a role - don't get me wrong. But missional communities will not grow unless there is a nurturing, sustaining presence prodding and investing for the long term. Leaders that can adapt, roll with the punches, and shepherd communally are more valuable than the high-powered "strong starters" who wish to be on to the next thing in two years.

These new kinds of leaders are mentored not through leadership conferences and books, but in regular times together to practice together listening and mutual submission. They need to see love and consistency, and they need guidance and not a dictator.

They Will Be Interpretive Leaders

Rarely do missional leaders lead their communities as the featured Bible teacher who dictates the Alpha and Beta of Biblical doctrine. Rather they are interpreters of what God is doing communally through the teaching and preaching of Scripture. They read Scripture in community and preach looking for what God is calling us to in the neighbourhood. It used to be that every church planter was a gifted preacher who could draw the crowds. Those days are past.

They are, not because you cannot attract dissatisfied or thrill seeking Christians from other churches with a great preacher, but because we have seen that true spiritual growth occurs communally only when the whole congregation is involved in times of praying, hearing, submitting and responding to the Word. Interpretive leaders[48] do not dictate from the pulpit a list of do's and don'ts and solutions from God for every problem. They interpret the Scriptures to open our eyes to what God is doing and where He is taking us. In other words, they cultivate other interpreters/listeners.

In a different way then, we must mentor leaders who are more than great preachers. They must lead their communities in seeing what God is doing via the eyeglass of Scripture. "Where is God taking us, where is he calling us?" How do we respond faithfully in this time and place?

The sermons and teaching of missional leaders, therefore, fund the corporate imagination of God's Kingdom in our midst and where He is at work in our everyday lives. And when conflicts arise, we sit and pray, submit to one another, and pray for courage and humility and discern the Scriptures for the journey we are in called to make in God's mission. This kind of leader often does not come from our (all too often) modernist seminaries. They are grown in a community which gathers to worship the Triune God so as to discern Him at work in our midst.

---

[48] I owe this term to my friend Jim VanYperen.

They Will Be Directors Of Spiritual Formation

I believe that missional leaders must know how to guide the community in spiritual formation. Admittedly, this kind of leadership is not common among younger evangelicals at least. Yet I still believe that the development of communal worship liturgies that are historically thick yet still local and organic is crucial for these times. We now recognize that the consumerist forces of our post Christendom Canada (and even worse in the United States) cannot be resisted as isolated individuals. An individual alone cannot resist the forces of desire that tell us a five bedroom house, and two new cars are more important than Mission, the very life we share with the Triune God. Our communities therefore must be places of spiritual formation, of resistance to the forces of distraction, unsatiated desire and exploitation of those we choose not to know.

This means that our Sunday/Saturday gatherings must be places of spiritual formation, encouragement and sending out for Mission. We must ever navigate against putting on a show that will attract; rather we must develop a liturgy that is simple, accessible and Scriptural and that guides our lives into Christ and guards us from the distractions that would take us away from Mission. I know that liturgy is a difficult pill to swallow these days for the newly arriving missional leaders. But there will be no missional community of people formed and shaped for mission if we just preach Mission as a legalistic requirement. Mission requires patience, a sense of vision and a level of self-denial that can only be formed inwardly in living bodies, trained in the simple organic disciplines/liturgies of the historic church.

They Will Be Leaders Who Give Away Power

Missional leaders that have served for any length of time have learned how to die to their egos and allow God to use every man and woman's gifts in the community for the furtherance of His Kingdom. Hierarchy is the product of Christendom. It hails to a day when Christianity still held power in society, when Jesus was still established as a given in Canada (even when the protestant liberal Jesus dominated Canada, there still remained a basis for authority and a respect for who Jesus was).

Hierarchy made sense in a day when the preacher in the town was looked up to and held power. This old world, when one man could wield influence and get things done in the name of Christ, is waning. As a result, no one man or woman can lead a community from the top down and expect the church to go on as a viable social reality. We cannot be the very Body of Christ if we do not empower the manifold gifts in the community to minister the kingdom as part of everyday life. If we even try to operate out of the old hierarchical ways, missional communities will flounder and their leaders will die from exhaustion. I have seen it happen over and over.

It is my belief therefore that missional leadership needs always to be multiple. Most missional pastors/leaders need to be bi-vocational (bi-ministerial) for their own survival. Such leaders must learn to mutually submit to the other leaders as they guide the journey of the community. They must mutually learn to mentor leaders and give away power. Different strengths should be recognized among leaders and then multiply that leadership[49].

This model subverts the CEO pastorate style we have all become so used to because each pastor gives away power instead of consolidating it. This kind of pastoral leadership models a living body for the rest of the community to see instead of dictating to the rest of the church to "just do it." In this way, all shall own the leadership of this community and the journey we are on in the Mission. This kind of leadership needs to be mentored, modelled and practiced and it never comes easy.

---

[49] Following the APEPT model of Frost and Hirsch in *The Shaping of Things to Come*. See also the work of Alan Roxburgh in *The Sky is Falling*.

	Functional 20th Century Church Technical Skills	Emerging Missional Church Adaptive Skills
Environment	• Stable • Predictable • Developmental	• Unstable • Discontinuous • Emergent
Organizational Culture	• Hierarchies • Bureaucracies • Managers/Experts • Top-down flow • Strategic Planning • Linear • Fragmentation	• Networks/Teams • Dialogue/Conscious Learning • Cultivated Diversity • De-Centered • Converging Conversations • Bottom-Up • Non-Linear • Integration
Leadership Functions	• Manage People • Optimize Performance • Control Structure	• Empower People • Nurture Teams • Invite Participation • Cultivate Environments

The Promise of Canada's New Missional Leaders and the Coming of Missional Orders

All of the above paints a picture of not just a new kind of leader, but also a new vision of what Canadian church can look like in post-Christendom. There is an invigorated ecclesiology emerging here in these up-and-coming church planters. This view of church places emphasis on forming a social life together that is rich in community. Inherent in this social life is the drive to be hospitable, open communities that invite the stranger into our midst, telling Our Story, ministering the grace and healing of the gospel. We will take up space, not as a defensive enclave, but as the visible manifestation of His reign ahead of time for all to see and experience.

This view of church says we must dedicate ourselves to a specific geographic area for many years at a time. We must inhabit this geography for Christ and discern where God is at work in those who cross our paths daily. We must look for the hurting and confused across this landscape, every day seeking to incarnate Christ to them. And we must patiently listen to our neighbours, blessing them and praying for their restoration.

Fresh+re:fresh

This long-term presence in our neighbourhoods makes mission to the lost within post-Christendom possible. This new sense of ecclesia knows we must live all of the above as a way of life born out of our relationship with the Triune God revealed in our Lord Jesus Christ. We must engage together in rhythmic transformational practices of spiritual formation that order our lives into God. Only in this way can we avoid becoming a new kind of social justice legalistic holiness. Many will recognize in this description some of the Rule of St. Benedict including the rule of *conversatio* (community), *hospitalitas* (hospitality), *stabilitas* (geography), and *obedientia* (transformative practices of mutual submission). This is the way of missional orders – an expression of kingdom life that can root missional communities in the new post-Christendom of the West.

Birthed out of this view of Christ's church, emerging missional leaders imbibe a mentality that is drastically different from the church planter of the past. They lead in ways more akin to an Abbot (or Abbess) of a Medieval missional order than an entrepreneurial wiz-kid of the typical franchise start-up church. They possess character like a patient gardener as opposed to the restless CEO numbers-cruncher. Indeed, most (not all) of the missional leaders I have met already exemplify strains of the new mentality. I believe this bodes well for the future. For I believe this new generation of pastors provides hope for a renewal of Christianity in Canada. They are already leading communities, house churches and monastic-like orders all over the country.

Like a fermenting revolution evolving out of a tired and reified ancien regime, these tiny bands of Christians have come on the scene committed to live a shared life of worship, spiritual formation, community, hospitality and service to the poor (of all kinds). In ways never imagined by the machinations of the evangelical mega-church, many of these bands are already infecting their neighbourhoods with an embodied gospel that cannot be denied -- only responded to.

Knowing Christendom is gone, these new leaders carry no pretension. Instead they embody the gospel in its most compelling, authentic, non-coercive form. This new wave of Christians is small in number and possesses little to no resources financially. Most do not impress with their grandiose visions. They do not hang in the halls of power. They do not make a show of their successes. Yet their vision of a simple Christian habitat as witness in the world reminds me of the Irish missional orders God used to effect a profound conversion of European society in the 4th century. We have seen the world changed like this once before (read How the Irish Saved Civilization, Thomas Cahill). Could we be in the early stages of seeing God move in a similar fashion once again? Let us pray it be so.

Fresh

Fresh

Planting New Expressions of Church

Rob Scott

Rob Scott has been the Community Director of King's Bridge since its inception in 1999. He has ministered in a diversity of settings including small Chipewyan villages in the North West Territories and migrant worker camps on the Baja Peninsula. Most of his work has been among the varied communities and personalities that make up inner city Calgary. Rob is an ordained minister in the Communion of Evangelical Episcopal Churches and is a provincially registered clergy person in Alberta. He currently lives in Calgary with his wife and twin daughters. More information about King's Bridge is available on their website, www.crossthebridge.ca.

Scaling the Church Walls
The Story of the King's Bridge Community

– Rob Scott

My name is Rob Scott, and I've been the community Director of King's Bridge since its inception in 1999.

I'd like to begin with a few questions. Who is a part of your congregation? What groups of people make up your parish? Who belongs to your faith community? Perhaps you're tempted to answer, "The people who go to my church."

But what if the answer to that question was inverted?

Everyone I encounter is a part of my parish. Everyone I congregate with, in any setting, is my congregation. As soon as I sit down to converse with someone, they've already entered my church.

This inversion is at the heart of the King's Bridge community. This shift underscores the journey we've been on for the past ten years, a journey forward that necessitates an appropriation of the past.

When I hear someone begin a conversation about churches with the phrase, "Fifty years ago…" my eyes glaze over and I start searching for the nearest exit. I expect a glowing portrait of the Western church's glory years to follow, and an indemnification of current cultural trends. I anticipate a grouchy editorial written via a very selective memory. But what you're about to read isn't going to glorify the white Anglo-Saxon Protestant past of Beaver-Cleaverdom. So bear with me through a short retrospective that begins with those infamous words.

Fresh

Fifty years ago the concept of the community parish was alive and well in many areas of Canada. There were a few small churches in each urban neighbourhood and ministers were known in the community. The sight of a man in a collar standing at a local market conversing with his neighbours was not strange. And even if you were in the minority and didn't attend church meetings, you knew where to go when you had spiritual questions. The church was an identifiable part of the community.

Of course there were all sorts of walls and barriers in this period as well. The sight of a woman in a collar would be shocking. The site of an Aboriginal, Oriental, African or South American in a collar would be novel. If a Catholic visited a Baptist church on a Sunday morning it would be a tale of political intrigue. And if you wore a turban or a *burka* in public in late October, odds are you were heading to a Halloween party rather than a temple or mosque.

One of the great developments of our current era is the disintegration of cultural homogeneity. But the era of post-Christendom in which we now live has also melted away the reality of the church as a vital participant in the community at large.

When I was in my mid-twenties, shortly after I was ordained, I conducted a funeral. I rarely wore a black suit, let alone a black shirt and clerical collar, but it was appropriate in this context for me to put on my uniform. So I did. Afterward, forgetting my costume, I made a quick stop at the grocery store. I paid for my items, turned to leave, and the man who'd bagged my groceries said to me, "Can I help you carry these to your car, Father?"

I was taken aback. I wanted Luke Skywalker to pop up from behind the counter and yell, "You're not my father!" We just don't live in the era of the community priest anymore. But maybe we should; maybe it's time for a covert operation. Maybe priests, pastors, congregants, deacons, blue-haired church ladies, sunny-faced Sunday school kids, upstanding board members, and slumbering bored members need to re-enter the community outside the church walls. Un-costumed, without recognition, position or authority, Christians can become a vital part of the community once again. This premise has piloted the King's Bridge community through several experiments and incarnations.

When King's Bridge began, our program structure defied the time-space continuum: It was the late '90s and we conducted Sunday services, child and youth ministry in a little white church building, surrounded by little white houses, attended mostly by little white people. Take away the TV screens in the sanctuary, and the rock-influenced music in the service, and you'd find yourself transported to 1952. The idea of the community parish was alive and well in our hearts and hopes. It was D.O.A. in our programs and priorities. Time travel wasn't a viable means of community connection. Almost no one outside of the Christian sub-culture was looking to churches as a point of connection.

So we began re-thinking. We looked at Acts 17:19 and asked ourselves, "Where is the Areopagus today?"

In the '50s the church was a community hub. Where are the community hubs today? Where do people connect beyond pre-established family, friendship and workplace relationships? What is the catalyst for these new connections? What is the core action involved in forming new bonds, new opportunities to share ideas, opinions and faith? And how do people begin to relate to each other across cultural and ideological divides?

Our search for community hubs brought us to cafés, pubs and university campuses.

Our search for the conduit for connection caused us to see the importance of conversation.

 And so we began searching for opportunities to relocate the life of our community from the little white church to campuses, pubs and cafes. We stopped trying to build services, songs and sermons, and started building conversations.

And we began looking for a home base from which to radiate these new efforts. For a year we pursued a new building of our own. The idea was to launch a storefront café with a small church sanctuary in a back room.

Fresh

We put every penny on the table, including my full salary. We turned every eyeball in our congregation in the direction of lease-able storefront spaces. We came very close to moving on a property before feeling that something was wrong. There was an indefinable sense of moving in the right direction, tainted by the wrong motives.

After much introspection, discussion, and missed opportunity we found a critical error in the core of our search. We were looking for a safe space. We were trying to rejuvenate the little white church idea by installing couches and coffee machines. We wanted to fabricate our own community hub rather than enter the post-Christian community hubs that already existed. We had control issues, and we lacked courage.

Redirected by this revelation, I began approaching owners of small, independent cafés near the University of Calgary. I pitched a program that included a weekly live music performance, and a discussion-starting short presentation. The café owners assumed we wanted to rent out their venue and use it for our program. They expected a private gathering that booked out their public space. It took some explanation on my part to convince them that we just wanted them to staff and run the café in the same manner they did every other day. We wanted the doors open; we wanted people to drop in. The band didn't mind if people came and went in the middle of the music. I didn't mind if they walked in or out in the middle of my presentation.

When we came to an agreement with a little café named the Double Mo, "come and go" is exactly what people did. I usually began by talking about a pop culture, political or social phenomenon. I then explored spiritual themes underlying this phenomenon. At the point I mentioned Jesus, I often witnessed a mini-exodus from the café. But others stayed and engaged the topic. Still more popped in after the music and message was done, diving into the conversations that had already begun.

Our band slowly replaced rock-infused Christian songs with spirit-infused secular songs. And their listeners began to hear Christian themes in the music they already loved and listened to on the radio.

I slowly replaced my pop-culture, three-point sermon model with a pop-culture three-question conversation catalyst. Disseminating religious answers from the stage wouldn't cut it in our community's new context, but stirring spiritual questions would.

Midway through the first year in our new café home, I discovered something hidden within myself; something that I hadn't seen clearly during my little white church years. It was something that had always been there, something dark, and broken. And I wasn't the lone sufferer of this disorder: it was hidden within many churches, ministers, and congregants. For me, this brokenness lived at the core of my past evangelistic efforts.

Throughout my early years of ministry I'd paid lip service to the idea of the Holy Spirit at work in the lives of "seekers." I'd tell people about times that I saw evidence of Christ revealing his presence to those outside of the church culture. I would say that I believed Jesus pursued people, wooed them, called them, and sometimes allowed Christians to be nearby as he was doing this. But in that dark broken place within myself I wasn't sure this was true. And it showed in everything I did, I just hadn't seen it.

How did it show? Years earlier, I'd been involved in a variety of evangelistic outreaches. I always made sure the keyboard was pumping out heart-tugging chords as I built towards my altar call. Throughout my life I'd engaged in many discussions about faith with those who had different beliefs. I always attempted to fortify and forward my seemingly intellectually sound apologetics. The brokenness was a subtle reliance on myself rather than Christ. I felt that it was up to me to introduce people to Jesus. I carried this burden as if God wasn't already active in other people's lives. It was up to me to make the connection. I was attempting to manipulate people toward faith. I was trying to convince them that I was right, and in so doing convince myself that I was right. I was afraid that if I went out into "the world" without my Christian posse and my emotional and intellectual conversion tools, I'd discover that Jesus wasn't really there. My driven, burdened attempts to convince people to follow Christ undermined his open, freeing attempts to do the same.

Let me pause here for a moment to say I don't believe every keyboard-fuelled altar call is manipulative. I don't believe every apologist is covering up his or her own lack of faith. I don't think these tools are inherently dark or broken, and I do think that most of the people who use them are faithful, loving people, who have much to teach me. I simply realized that they were crutches for me, in my ministry situation, at that time.

Venturing out into a context where these tools were inappropriate was necessary in order for me to see that Jesus is alive and active in the world at large, with or without me. I needn't be burdened with the mandate of enticing people to follow him. I could, however, follow him as he moved through the markets, meetings and menageries of our world and demonstrated his presence to those who had not yet turned their attention to him. I could enter the conversations he had already begun.

One evening at the Double Mo, I began talking with a new employee behind the counter before having to leave the conversation to jump up on the stage for the evening's presentation. During the presentation I spoke of my faith. I had been outed. As I re-entered the earlier conversation, the young man repositioned himself into a "talking to a Christian" mode. He quite brashly, and outside of the context of our discussion, declared that he was an atheist. I asked him how he'd found himself in this position.

He fumbled around for a while and eventually told me that when he was a teenager, his family had attended church regularly. It had been a liberal mainline denominational congregation. He told me that he once approached the minister with questions of faith. One of the questions was, "What's the point of attending church?" He was told the purpose of the church was to allow people to come together to be comforted. They could gather together and have their worldview affirmed and feel safe from the struggles of life. He told me that in his experience this comfort was a false-panacea and he had too many questions and ideas to tolerate church anymore.

I told him that I shared some of his feelings. I felt the church should agitate as much as it comforts. It should be asking as many questions as it's answering. It should stir things up. He came alive at this idea. He said he'd definitely attend a church like that. For the next couple of months, he stood behind the counter with new questions churning inside him. On occasion, he joined me for a beer after work, and our conversation continued. And as far as I know, he never realized that he was at church the whole time. He never acknowledged that he'd found himself in our parish. Or perhaps our parish had found itself in him.

Our time at the Double Mo also accelerated our activities in social justice causes. We had worked on projects dealing with HIV/AIDS for some time. And then one evening the pandemic became much more personal.

A young South African couple was in town for several speaking engagements. On Sunday evening they would be speaking at King's Bridge's café gathering. Throughout the week leading up to this, my wife and I visited with them, introduced them to downhill skiing, and grew to really enjoy their company. They were a lot like us. They had experienced the love of Christ. They wrestled with the culture of mainstream Christianity. They were enjoying the early years of their marriage. But unlike us, they were both HIV positive. He in fact, had developed a full expression of AIDS and had nearly died before being accepted for a research trial of anti-retroviral drugs.

The café was packed on the evening they spoke. They shared simply from their experience. They shared insightfully about the situation in South Africa. They shared their faith. They shared themselves.

When they finished, I stepped up onto the stage and found myself staring into a room full of teary eyes. I didn't know what to say. And so I did something I never thought I'd do corporately in the café. I invited those gathered to join me in prayer. Atheists, Muslims, Christians and the religiously undeclared joined together in those few moments, because God had walked through the room and brushed up against us. God had revealed himself through this young couple.

That evening changed King's Bridge. One of our members went to work with children with HIV/AIDS in Romania. Another stepped into an ongoing role as an emissary of our community in Africa; for several years now, she has worked in South Africa and Uganda with adults and children struggling with HIV/AIDS.

When we climbed over the little white church walls and adopted the community at large as our congregation, social justice issues ceased to be distant causes: they became practical realities. Since our exodus from the

Fresh

insular, mainstream church model we have always had members of our community who live on the street, members who struggle with mental illness, members pushed to the fringes of society. These situations aren't political issues, they're family struggles for our community.

After a year, The Double Mo closed its doors; another victim of the current love-affair with the Mega-McStarbucks juggernaut. We were only given six days notice of the closure: six days until our next event; six days to see if God had any creative energy he wanted to pour into our void. In those six days, we were invited to move to another café, a shop named Soma. We didn't need to knock on office doors or make a pitch to owners or try to sell ourselves. Amrit, a Hindu woman and Darim, her Sikh husband owned Soma. After we relocated to their venue, they attended almost every one of our events. They even brought their children. And while I had many vital conversations with others during our time at Soma, the deepest conversations about Christ were with them. Family considerations caused them to sell the café after we had spent a year there. When I said goodbye to them, I told Darim something very personal, not knowing how he would respond or whether I might even offend him. I told him that when I envisioned God the Father in my mind, it was Darim's face I saw. His response was a teary-eyed embrace.

During our time at Soma we realized there was a cultural barrier in our program. While people of widely varied ages, worldviews, ethnicities and economic castes were able to find some degree of connection with the King's Bridge community, there was one group that found themselves excluded: young families. This exclusion was one of pragmatics not intent. A conversational café can't accommodate the interests and energy of small children unless it is equipped for them. The Double Mo wasn't child-friendly. Soma was child-friendly, but not well equipped. And King's Bridge's events were neither child-friendly nor child-equipped.

As these observations rattled around in my cranium, I began to envision a business venture. It was an idea I wasn't well positioned to pursue myself, but it seemed strange that a city of a million people hadn't yet seen it develop. There were coffee shops with small play areas for children. But what if a café was to open with a huge play area and a small quiet zone for parents to sip and chat? One day, as my wife and I drove past a vacant commercial building, we talked about how perfect it would be for this sort of venture. The next week a new tenant started renovating. A couple of month's later, they put up a sign that read "Coffee and S'cream: A Full Service Coffee Spot With Separate Area For Parent And Tot." I was floored; and excited. The next day I contacted the owners to set up a meeting to try to sell them on a new King's Bridge program. It took six months, a handful of phone calls and three meetings, but eventually they agreed to a trial program. We called it Kid's Bridge.

Kid's Bridge, much like our other café ventures, primarily attracted people from outside of the church culture. While many were sporadic in their attendance, connections deepened with several families who attended Kid's Bridge regularly. Each event was a combination of playtime for the children and discussion time for the parents. The subject matter of our discussions was usually practical and parenting-oriented. Spiritual themes were introduced as a handful of parents and I simply shared our experiences and perspectives.

One evening, a father who regularly attended approached me outside of the parent's discussion. It was clear something was on his mind. As we began to talk, he shared that he felt he had a role in nurturing his children's faith. He had Catholic roots, but hadn't attended church in many years. He wasn't sure what he believed himself, and now he found himself responsible for two little people full of questions. The weight of his struggle was apparent. This was a difficulty that he hadn't articulated to anyone before. When spiritual and identity issues collide, people sometimes find themselves with no one to talk to. Paralyzed and guilt-ridden, they feel that God is an adversary rather than an ally. I suggested that there were several simple exploratory steps he could begin to take both for himself and his children's questions. As the conversation progressed I could see the weight lifting from his face. Near the end of the evening it became clear that he had begun to explore the idea that God could be an intimate partner in parenting, rather than a distant judge.

During the first year of the Kid's Bridge program, Darim and Amrit, the Soma owners, experienced a family situation that compelled them to sell the café. They asked the new owner to continue to host our gathering and he agreed to do so, saying that he would give us at least a month's notice if he changed plans. The day he gained possession of the café, he reneged on his promise and told us we would no longer be able to meet at Soma. This time we found ourselves with only three days notice: three days until our next event; three days that would catch me off-guard by challenging and changing bigotry I hadn't realized lay within me.

When we launched into café-based ministry, we intentionally sought out secular locations. On occasion I would say to church-phobic acquaintances, "Why don't you come to church and I'll buy you a beer." The secular, licensed locations we gathered in went a long way toward dissipating the Christian stereotypes that kept people from connecting. Shortly after we began pursuing our first café location, a very large church in Calgary started a café of its own. It was called The House Coffee Sanctuary. To my jaded eyes, it seemed like a hangout for the church's youth and young adult groups, rather than an open community connection point. When it opened, Christian music populated its sound system, alcohol was banned from its menu, local affluent condo-dwellers seemed more welcome than local homeless people, and the young people gathered were of the suburban evangelical variety rather than the urban neo-hippy variety that lived near the café.

Of course, this perspective was only partly founded in reality. As a salve for my own identity and faith struggles, I had embraced a bigoted perspective toward mainstream Christianity. It's the same prejudice that lingers in the darker corners of a handful of emergent and missional church communities. It was a blinder that kept me from seeing a remarkable evolution happening at the church-owned café in question.

When King's Bridge was faced with eviction from the Soma café, I desperately looked around for a café to host our next event and came up short. And then I swallowed my pride and called up the pastor/manager of The House Café. He immediately welcomed us to move our event to his venue. He had taken the reins of the café in its second year of operation, after I had already formed my opinion of the place.

Under his management, the evangelical majority had declined, and the indigenous urbanites of the area had been embraced. Several homeless people had found connection through the café and received assistance in getting off the street and dealing with other issues. A new, open, conversational atmosphere had emerged—an atmosphere that embraced the diversity of perspectives found in the culture-at-large. The programs at the café, which had initially been run by its mother church, had given way to gatherings run by a variety of grass-roots community and faith organizations. The House had been transformed from a mainstream church outpost to a true community hub. In short, the café was now modelling much of what King's Bridge desired to become, and all that prevented a meaningful partnership was my attitude.

The prejudice revealed to me through The House's transformation led me to re-assess my disconnection from church culture in general. I began to seek out other communities that were asking the same questions as King's Bridge. I discovered there were a handful of churches on similar journeys. Moreover, I discovered that there were a handful of individuals within even the most stalwart evangelical circles that were moving beyond the walls of their communities. Jargon is often more polarizing than illuminating. But for better or worse, my reconnection with other churches brought me into "the emerging church conversation," and gave me the term "missional" to describe the efforts of the King's Bridge community.

Over the years we've continued to change and stretch as we seek to connect. We've moved our band into stand-alone evening gigs. I've dropped my spoken word presentations and begun to hit the streets with a video camera. Rather than trying to introduce a conversation in the café, I now go out and start having the conversation on the street. I have it in a pot-smoke-laced, open courtyard two blocks away from The House; I have it across the street in front of the tattoo parlour; I have it with the window shoppers around the corner. It happens in the New Age bookstore down the street, and I capture snippets of it on film and bring it back to the café and it grows from there. It grows online through our bridgetalk.ca website, and spins off into several other web conversations outside of our site: sometimes even outside of our awareness. It grows in the café and spins off into several other physical conversations outside of our meeting place, and it grows in ways we can't possibly fabricate or sustain. No matter; the One who fabricated the universe can, and does, sustain us all.

The handful of personal interactions I've described here are emblematic of the connections we find ourselves making through our church community. Those who would call themselves King's Bridgers are few, but the conversations are many. We often come alongside people at the beginning of an emerging dialogue with God; sometimes we even get to help catalyze that conversation. On rare occasion we've been able to see that catalytic process through from its initiation to the point where someone more fully enters the embrace of Christ. The moments of decision are wonderful, but it's the early part of the spiritual journey that we've gravitated towards. It's the initial life questions that compel people to pursue Christ we find most compelling.

Fewer and fewer people in Canada have Christian roots to draw on. While the number of people initiated into the church sub-culture drops, the number of people longing for connection keeps growing. It's growing inside cozy cafés and on chilly street corners, online and offline, in relationships and in solitude. The longing is drawing together a new kind of congregation, a new kind of parish, one that can't be enumerated or homogenized. This new community may seem hostile to church culture, but it's open to Christ. It may seem uninterested in joining the church community, but it's open to the church community joining it. It may seem ephemeral, but it's captivated by the eternal. It may seem disembodied, but I believe it is the body of Christ.

Kim Reid

Kim Reid has been involved in youth work and ministry for thirty years. From 1978 to 1992, Kim worked professionally with Emotionally Disturbed Adolescents. Kim has been in full-time ministry for sixteen years. He began The Vault, a drop-in centre for teens, under YFC. In 1996 he started On Rock Ministries, under whose umbrella The Vault continues to grow and thrive. On Rock has expanded into community services, and as such is operating a food bank and a lunch program for under privileged elementary school kids.

Kim has has been involved in the Canadian music scene since 1982, most notably with the band Innocent Blood from 1985 to 1995. Kim continues to be involved in the music scene, mentoring musicians and promoting Hard-Core shows.

Kim and Sylvia have been married for twenty-two years and have three amazing kids. Kirstyn is seventeen, Kayla is fifteen and Josh is twelve. Their family also includes many other people, too numerous and shy to mention.

Kim and some friends planted The Open Door community Church in 2004. Kim blogs at www.lifecycleproject.org.

The Open Door

– Kim Reid

My name is Kim Reid, I was born in Kingston, ON, but have spent most of my life in the Montreal area. I was born into a family that did not place any importance on following Jesus, so I was introduced to Jesus through foster parents. My only experience with church before that time was occasionally attending an Anglican church, whose minister had an affection for alcohol and picked his sermons out of a file right before the morning service. Kids ate toast and peanut butter in the front rows, and men read the paper in the back. It was a vibrant little church (not). We used to steal snow shovels and store them in the church boiler room. The janitor could never figure out why he had fifteen shovels.

My last experience in a foster home was with Christian (Pentecostal) foster parents. I was twelve, and not very interested in church. They didn't force me and my brother to go to church, and somewhere along the line this made me curious. When I finally began going, I was pretty freaked out by the expressiveness of the people. There was a lot of cultural real estate between my little Anglican church and this massive Pentecostal church.

I have never fit in to the church culture: even when I was in my early teens, I always felt a little outside. When I was young, I thought this outside feeling was a bad thing. I tried to fit in, but I'm not very good at faking it. I never quite understood the fortress mentality of many evangelical churches. They seem to be protecting themselves from my friends and family, who weren't that dangerous.

Fresh

I skipped around denominations a lot in my late teens and developed what I called back then a denominational tolerance and appreciation. I would say that if we could take the good from most denominations and put them together we might have a pretty amazing church.

After high school, I began working with marginalized people – first with the intellectually handicapped, and later on with juvenile delinquents. I had always sensed that I would be in full time ministry, but I didn't know what that would look like because I did *not* want to be a pastor. Back in the early 70s, if you were in ministry, you were a pastor.

In my experience working with delinquents, I started to envision being an influence in kids lives before they were "in the system." Eventually I started dreaming about a drop-in centre idea.

In 1986, I married Sylvia. In 1991, God made it clear to us that it was time to move into the next chapter of our lives. I made it clear to him that he needed to tell Sylvia this as well. Turned out he was already doing it. I approached YFC with this drop-in centre idea, only to find out that they operated a few such centres across Canada. Why reinvent the wheel? The process of joining YFC began.

In 1992, The Vault opened and I was in ministry heaven. Little did I know that God was having fun.

Through the Vault, we have seen many lives change, most for the better. We have watched "kids" grow in faith and become true Jesus followers. Some of them have gone into full time ministry.

I realized from the beginning that the key to reaching people and changing lives was long term involvement, and that meant we needed staff that would stick around. The average drop-in staff stay at the time was about six months. We decided that our staff would need to be a cohesive group of people with a single minded purpose, and a sense that they were in this together. So, we became a family; we poured our lives into each other. We played, prayed, laughed and cried together; we loved each other and our kids, and the kids knew it. We began referring to ourselves as "the community."

We would work the drop-in on Friday and Saturday nights, and hang out at my house on Sunday nights. We would watch movies, eat, play games and just have fun. This became known as the open house at Kim & Syl's. After a while other people started showing up, with things like, "I heard there was an open house here tonight: is anybody welcome?" Sometimes we didn't even know the people. We had to change the format because we couldn't afford to feed thirty people every week. So, we would get people to bring ingredients for the "meal." Syl would decide what we were going to eat. People would phone in and she would tell them what component to bring and the meal would come together.

Somewhere along the way, people started feeling the need for more than just movies and games. People started talking about worshipping on Sunday nights before food and movies. Somehow this need for God and for a spiritual centre began to come out. We responded by pulling out a few guitars and worshipping. A few months later, people started expressing the need for sharing Scripture and learning. We pulled out some Bibles and started sharing Scripture together.

I have always been frustrated with the chasm that exists between my reality in the world with the people I hang with and the sub-culture of the church. As I spent more and more time with unchurched people, I realized that our little world made no sense outside of the church walls. This is why people don't want to be a part of our churches; it makes no sense in the real world. As our ministry grew the church world made less sense to me as well.

At this point I was an elder in a church with Brethren roots. The church was quite progressive for an evangelical church, but still did not connect with the people we were meeting.

In 2002, a little before Christmas, I asked our Sunday night group what they got out of church. All thirty of us had the same answer: nothing. Our church was a family experience and a part of our lives. It was where we met each other, and began our day together. But in that other formal expression, people weren't connecting with the music or the message being communicated. So, why get up at 9am to be at church for 11am, when you only went to bed at 3am?

Fresh

While this was going on, I was getting the sinking feeling that we were a church already. I began to wonder if God had played a sick joke on me, and had created a church while I wasn't paying attention.

Early in 2003, we received an invitation to a church planting congress in Vancouver and we decided to attend. There was a seminar on house churches and Syl chose to attend. She was not very open to the idea that we were already a church. When she found me after the seminar, her first words were, "we are a church." Apparently the guy had a check list of things house churches do and we were doing all of them.

All this to say, we did not decide to plant a church, as most people do. We didn't plan or strategize, and we didn't follow a "how-to" manual. We grew into a community of believers and non-believers as we journeyed together, trying to figure out how to walk with Jesus in this messed up world. This Jesus thing can be very subversive.

My Theology:

I believe the Bible to be the word of God. I do not doubt its authenticity. I do however, question our interpretation of it.

The evolution in my theology only began as I stepped outside of the church in a real way to build relationships in the unchurched world. As I made friends and shared life, I realized that the theology I had been taught made me uncomfortable. It did not make sense outside of the church walls.

As I took a hard look at the life of Jesus, I realized that He did not, and could not, play by the rules we had set up as "The Church." Jesus wasn't a "peace at all costs" kind of guy. He wasn't as concerned about our comfort as we are. Jesus didn't just give a yearly offering to "the poor," they were his friends. He genuinely liked all the people we look down on, hanging out with criminals and hookers and tax collectors and poor people. In "the Church," the formal church, our reason for being seemed to be to protect ourselves from the world Jesus lived in.

As we made attempts at integrating our friends into the existing church, we realized that at the end of the day, they did not understand this sub-culture we were involved in. Most of the time we walked away embarrassed, and our friends were confused. The problem was that the church didn't reflect us or the God we shared with our friends. It simply was not welcoming or hospitable to those who didn't fit the culture. They felt judged and they felt shunned.

We slowly became more comfortable with our unchurched friends than we did with church people. The world had valid questions, and the church had very few acceptable answers, and were unwilling to admit the grey areas. We are shared some confusing with some of what God says and does. To this day we do not have all the answers; God is bigger than our theologies. I do not even like some of what God says, but -- He is God. I have to walk in faith sometimes, and I hate it. But I love God, and I am learning to trust Him.

My view of what church "is" was changed as we started to become a community. I began to notice that our community looked a whole lot more like the stuff Paul spoke of regarding the church than did our local church on the corner. We knew each other; we ate together; we were in each others lives. Issues like discipline became easier to manage because we were friends and reconciliation was the goal, not protecting ourselves from the blemish of sin. Remember Willard's "Gospel of sin management"?

As we learned to journey with each other and with God, we realized that our view of salvation was messed up. We were called to make disciples, not save people. Making disciples takes a long time; it is an investment. We had to start seeing people as God saw them; we needed to see them as dearly loved by God -- His creation. So, we needed to "let them in." We realized that people needed to belong, so that they could believe. This may not be the case for everyone, but it seems to be the way it is for many of those we have met. So, now we have a guy who has done way too many drugs, sleeping it off on our sofa during a Sunday night open house. We learn to deal with a guy who drinks too much at our gatherings, and teach him how to drink responsibly and follow Jesus. It is messy, but it is real, and lives are changing.

I don't argue theology anymore. I am interested in deep water issues. What are my non-negotiables?

Jesus. To be a follower of Jesus, you need to be following, no matter how slowly. What did Jesus say and what did He do? Am I following in these things and doing them? Jesus cared about the poor a whole lot more than most Christians would like to admit. He made taking care of the poor a major criteria for salvation, and the only criteria for judgment (Matthew 25). I had never been taught this at any church I attended. It was always about looking good and holy on Sunday, keeping up the appearance of perfection. I had to come to grips with, "does Jesus inhabit my being, or does church?"

In many ways the Bible is a much harder book than we have made it out to be, and at the same time, much simpler as well. It isn't rocket science. I think we have made it more complicated, so that we would not have to deal with its difficulty.

The Open Door has been functioning officially for four years. We average about thirty at our celebration at the moment, however, we have another twelve to fifteen hardcore kids who do a study with me on Monday nights. They even find The Open Door daunting.

There are also those who are on the periphery of our community, those who are trying to figure out life and faith. They seem to want to be close, but not personal. Altogether there are probably between 75 and 100 people connected to our community. There are many who think we are a young people's church, because of who I am and the activities we embrace, however, we have quite a wide age range, much like typical church demographics. We have a lot of people in their 20s and 30s, and we also have people from 50 to 80. Bill and Bessie are in their late 70s, early 80s. They say they come to the OD because the spirit of God's peace is here. We have had several weddings in the past four years, and so little children are becoming more numerous.

People who may feel marginalized in an average evangelical church, find their way to the OD as well. We have a few mentally ill people and a few alcoholics in our community. Everyone is welcome. Victor is a man in his 60s. He is an alcoholic and has no desire to stop drinking. He also loves Jesus. Sometimes Victor is more like Jesus than most people I know: he is always helping and taking care of others. There is no job too menial for Victor; he is a part of our community.

When we decided to have a corporate meeting at The Vault (our drop-in centre), we had to decide what made sense, in terms of activity. What do we do at this meeting? We chose to do three things.

The first was to eat together. This is very important to us. Eating helps create community. The sharing of food is universal. No matter what background or culture you come from, food is a shared experience. I would argue that this is the most important aspect of our celebration. We have a community pot, every week someone agrees to bring food for the next week. Whoever takes the pot, brings it back full the next week, and that is what we share. Soup, chili, salads, and bbq's in the summer are favourites.

We are a community that is very musical; we have a very rock'n'roll heritage and many who appreciate the hardcore scene. I believe that worship needs to be indigenous, to come from within the community. To this end, a worship music experience was a need for us. So, we have a time of worship which looks a lot like a concert. It is very chaordic. To a visitor, it may seem totally disorganized.

We have several very good musicians, but they are musicians at heart. For someone used to professional worship leaders, this might be daunting. We have an open mic, which allows anyone who wants to, to join the band on any given song. Sometimes, that means an amazing harmony happens, other times it means the sound man has to turn the mic off. It allows kids, mentally challenged people, amazing singers and tone deaf people all to feel a part of the worship. Sam can get up to the mic with his hoodie up and do his best hip-hop moves without ever singing a word, but he is in the moment and it is meaningful. Some days it is pretty ordinary: the band leads and nothing crazy happens, but we worship.

The third component is "teaching". My personal view is that teaching comes from within community: we all learn from each other. We all have stuff to learn and teach. This segment is more of an open forum facilitated by the person up front. Sometimes it looks like a semi-normal teaching session, only with heckling. Other times it can turn into a full on argument, and it looks like the wheels are coming off. I pay attention to the ebb and flow of our community. What are people dealing with? What are our struggles? How are we relating to each other and the world around us? Are there issues of faith that we need to address? Jesus is a big deal. How do we walk in this world and walk with Jesus at the same time? What does it mean to follow Jesus? In past year we have been focusing on the words of Jesus, trying to understand what was important to Him.

On paper, our gathering can look a lot like a "typical" church gathering; however, most people find the experience quite different. We are not seeking to be emerging, or postmodern, or post-postmodern. We are striving to be real and live out our life with Jesus in a way that touches our world and changes lives.

Leadership is a hot button issue today in church development. I am pretty sure God is more interested in servant-hood. I am definitely the leader in our community, but, I am a part of the community. This is my family and we are friends.

Decisions within our community are made by people in the community. We have an informal structure for the most part, where whoever is in the room at the time of a decision, has a say. Anyone can have a say. Even our neighbour , who is not "interested" at all in faith, has given input on some church decisions, because she was there and we asked what she would do. My kids, who are sixteen, fourteen, and eleven, have had input into decisions, because they are a part of the community and may see things from a different perspective. We learn from each other. On rare occasions, someone has to have the final say. In those instances it would be in my lap, but these are rare cases.

Financial decisions are made by a semi-formal committee, because we are a part of the Free Methodist Church in Canada. However, the three members of this committee are a part of the community and therefore understand the heart of the community.

When you put a group of people in a room with no leadership structure and assign a task, in most cases, a structure will be created naturally. If the task is technical, then technical people will have the reins. If the task is financial, then the bankers will rise to the occasion. This is what happens in community. You learn what gifts and talents people bring to the table and when the need arises, you let them run with it. This way, people feel appreciated and a genuine part of the community. I have very little understanding of finances. Show me a spreadsheet, and I will slip into a coma. I don't get it. So, when it comes to that stuff, my wife and others run the show. I ask questions and trust my family members to manage the rest. I am the same way with computer technology.

In my opinion, leadership comes down to trust. If we can trust each other, then I don't have to control everything (Think, "The Speed of Trust").

The Open Door is a part of the Free Methodist Church in Canada. When we were trying to figure this whole church thing out, I was approached by Jared Siebert, who at the time was a pastor at Next in Kingston, about becoming part of FMC. I later met with Dan Sheffield and explained that I needed three things from FMC. First, I needed to be involved with a community of similar church leaders who understood where I was coming from. Second, I needed money. Third, I wanted to be left alone to do what God was calling us to. I did not want a denomination to try to control something they didn't understand. All three of my conditions were accepted. So far, I am thrilled with the community and the hands off aspects of our arrangement. The financial part has been a struggle, due to available funding, however, FMC is doing what it can, and we continue to trust God for the rest. We are blessed to be able to do what we feel God has called us to.

Most of my mentors are dead, or they are movie characters. My father-in-law, Joe Kass, is definitely up there. He is 72, and never stops learning. He has watched our community grow with some skepticism, and has become a full on part of it. He continues to live life to the fullest, while dealing with a cancer that should have claimed him two years ago. He trusts God and loves life. He is a grandfather to my kids and our community. When he was skeptical, he watched, without criticism. When he saw the fruit, he rejoiced rather than rationalize.

I love Wesley, but I recognize that he was not Jesus. He was as messed up as the rest of us, but he was relentless in his passion for God and the poor.

Fresh

C.S. Lewis was a genius. He was postmodern long before the word was invented and if half the people who idolized him actually understood his writing, they would call him a heretic.

John McLane, A solution oriented, passionate man, who was willing to do whatever it took to get the job done and save those he loved. John Constantine and William Wallace are up there as well.

I guess the bottom line for me is that planting churches may be the wrong goal: building community is the place to start. Many church plants fail, due to disagreements, vision, etc. Most church planters recruit a core group. However, if these people are not invested in each other, if they don't become family, then when times get tough, when differences occur, people leave. In building community, we build lasting relationships. It isn't always pretty; more often than not it is messy, but it is real. "Church" should not be about worship style, targeting people groups, or any of those things. It should be about walking together, celebrating God in our lives and loving our neighbours.

I have been asked many times how we do what we do at The OD. I can tell people what we do, but I cannot provide a formula to be copied; neither can anyone else. Every community is different. We have different needs, personalities, neighbours and contexts. Trying to duplicate a system for what the church is supposed to be, doesn't work. In this sense, community grows out of the context of the mission and I think our record proves that. We will continue to be and build community, learning what it means to follow Jesus and love this world that God created, together.

Scott Cripps

Scott is a restless thirty-one year old. He loves venturing out into the great unknown and being a part of new things. Currently this involves Awaken, and FAME (www.fameassets.com), a new, cutting-edge company. He is married to a beautiful hippie – Leanne – who fosters an organic, environmental, alternative existence for Scott and their three girls. Their daughters are Hannah, seven; Ella, four; and Lily, three. The Cripps live in a beautiful neighbourhood in Calgary called Bowness where they try to love their neighbours and contribute to community life. Scott's restlessness contributes to his involvement with sports in football, and coaching soccer for his girls.

Scott blogs at www.publicpondering.typepad.com and Awaken is found at www.awaken-online.com.

The Story of Awaken

– Scott Cripps

"You'll look up and down streets"

My name is Scott Cripps and I pastor Awaken. Awaken is a question-formed community. We ask honest questions and we are seeking honest answers. Often we can ask questions where we already assume we know the answers, or we can ask questions where regardless of the answers we are going to stick to a given path. For Awaken, as it was for Neo in the over-quoted and over-metaphored movie, "The Matrix" – "It's the question(s) that drives us".

Certainty is a tempting mistress and without questions we often fall back to the place where we feel the most secure, the place where we are the most familiar. So it is with much humility that I write this, because Awaken has not arrived yet... in fact we are still very much in the process of discerning, listening and asking. This chapter will provide a snapshot of Awaken, a small community of believers in the northwest corner of Calgary who are striving to be faithful to the calling God has placed on us.

"It's opener there in the wide open air"

Awaken has been a work of God. There is no other way to understand it. In fact, there is no other way we should ever understand the Church. As much as technique, personality and charisma can attract a crowd to form a community, the church's roots, foundation and ongoing work on earth is based in the very heart of God who desires His people to gather, demonstrate and proclaim His transformative power. This heartbeat of Jesus is what Awaken is trying to encompass.

Awaken began as a third service of a contemporary Baptist (CBWC Baptist) church in NW Calgary. It was originally designed to attract and reach postmodern folks who weren't likely to darken the doorway of a traditional church service in the morning. In order to accomplish this it went down the pathway of 'experiential worship' where each Sunday there needed to be some sort of element of participation, or creative expression, or just things done different.

It was into this situation that I entered the equation. I was serving as the youth pastor at this church and eventually my role grew to include Awaken and with Awaken, God drew together a community where we could learn and listen together. It wasn't long into this experience that I realized that living under the umbrella of an established church wasn't allowing us to risk, venture and really grow into what God was calling us to be. I felt initially that Awaken was simply 'playing church' and had yet to take steps towards really understanding what it meant to be the Church. It was at this point that we began to ask questions such as 'What is the gospel', 'What is the Church', 'What is the kingdom' and 'what does justice look like?' It was also at this point that we began to dream, pray and discern where the missio dei was going to lead us.

I never really saw myself as a church planter; in fact while going to university, I didn't really envision myself as a pastor. I stumbled into the ministry through the back door as staffing changes had caused an opening within the youth ministry and I was hired to run the programs as a part time job while I finished my degree in political science from the University of Calgary.

But God had other ideas. He kept bringing mentors, authors, teachers and friends into my life, and the result was a community formed and launched into the neighbourhood of Bowness. Awaken is a community that is willing to turn from comfortable existence in a larger church, to being homeless and relying on the hospitality of others. We are a community that is willing to embrace the unknown together and to keep asking questions.

"You'll start happening too"

My journey of leading and participating with Awaken down this pathway to a missional existence in a new neighbourhood is the result of a number of factors. New imagination is needed to venture out into the unknown and for myself this new imagination came together (and is coming together) by seeking and listening to voices among and beyond ourselves. It is easy to live within the comforts of your own reality; it is a greater challenge to be open to moving beyond the limits of your experience. There are the two major factors that provided impetus to Awaken taking steps towards becoming a missional community.

First of all, God brought together a willing and passionate group of people. Community has been a key for us. Personally my wife (Leanne) and daughters (Hannah, Ella, and Lily) felt God calling us to live a simple life among folks who are different than us in a neighbourhood that had a diverse reality to it. But we gained courage and resolve when this vision was shared beyond ourselves into our community and others were willing to venture out with us. It is through these relationships we have with each other that we've been able to become something we are not by ourselves.

One story of Awaken's resolve and blessing was to release my family and I on a seven-month leave of absence right at the point where we had decided to commit to being a church plant. A number of folks who heard that I was going to be stepping away asked who was going to replace me and preach while I was gone. They were asking that question rooted in an ecclesiology where only a trained clergy could lead, preach and guide a community. Fortunately Awaken had long since grown beyond that imaginative limit, and not only remained afloat but actually deepened the sense of community and commitment to our vision.

This experience of stepping away resulted in us all learning a number of invaluable lessons that we couldn't have learned if my family and I did not relinquish the role of being the sole owner of the vision. We learned that the Spirit of God does reside in his people and in doing so gifts and equips everyday folks to contribute and lead in cultivating an expression of God's church. We learned that who we are and what abilities and resources we have are not merely adequate but are powerful enough to demonstrate God's transformative power. We learned that leadership is not one person who knows all and does all, but rather occurs as a relational process among people. And finally we learned that through the ups and downs, the challenges and victories, God is good.

The second major factor in Awaken's impetus was that God began to bring people into my life that in each their own way began to cultivate and help me to see a bigger picture. The following are these people:

The first was my theology professor at Canadian Theological Seminary. His name is Mabiala Kenzo. Kenzo was the first person who put the book, "The Missonal Church" by Guder into my hands. It was under his teaching and tutelage that I saw a much bigger picture of the church and how it has been forming over the centuries by various traditions. I took every theology course I could at CTS including a course in 'Narrative Theology' that added depth to my understanding of Scripture. As a Christian I first acknowledged my conversion and relationship with Jesus when I was a child but with Kenzo, a second conversion occurred: a love for the Church and for God's mission through the Church into the world. I realized that despite people's sentiments, you cannot love Jesus and hate the Church. They cannot be separated. It was with this ecclesial foundation that I became passionate about cultivating a community where we could ask, "what is the Church' and then pursue the vision together.

The second person that God brought into my life was Cam Roxburgh. Cam is the pastor of Southside Community Church in the lower of mainland of B.C. and the head of Church Planting Canada. It was at a church planting conference in Toronto in 2005 that Cam and I met and it was there that Cam extended an invitation to my family to come out to Vancouver and to see and experience Southside first hand.

Awaken gave us with their blessing and in December of 2006 we arrived in Vancouver. During my time at Southside I was able to join a community that had incarnated the gospel into five different neighbourhoods and I was able to witness the character and competencies of the leaders who were leading Southside into these neighbourhoods. I saw the power of a covenant that held everyone together and focused folks on the task that God had called them to. I saw the amazing ability of everyday folk to be mentored into leadership and then lead communities into their missional existence, and finally I saw the heart of missional leaders and their love for God, each other and their neighbourhoods.

The third person that God had brought across my path was someone who has known me since the day I was born. It is my uncle Bob Swann. My uncle Bob and Aunt Anne have always been heroes to me. They have spent the majority of their adult lives living out the mission of God to folks in Kenya and Somalia, as well as to refugees in Toronto and homeless folks on the downtown eastside of Vancouver. When we ventured out to Vancouver to connect with Southside, it was my Uncle Bob and Aunt Anne who opened their home to my family and welcomed us in. Living with them we were exposed to people whose heart beat for the marginalized, the poor, the refugees and the sick. I was exposed to an aspect of the gospel that I had not explored nor had I seen up close. While living with uncle Bob, my family and I were surrounded by stories of God's kingdom breaking into the midst of folks who were living in the toughest of circumstances and was invited to experience that reality by accompanying my uncle on a number of occasions through the streets of Vancouver and to the shelter he ran through 1st Baptist Church Vancouver.

Through these three voices, theology, neighbourhood and justice began to become the primary ingredients in what God was cooking with Awaken. Each of these lenses allowed me to see beyond the limits of my own vision and to catch a glimpse of a more holistic gospel and ecclesiology.

"You will come to a place where the streets are not marked"

In September of 2007, Awaken began to gather on Sunday evenings in the neighbourhood of Bowness in the NW of Calgary. Unlike most of Calgary, Bowness is a very old and established neighbourhood. It once existed as its own town prior to being engulfed as part of Calgary in the 1960s. It is not a monochromatic community where everyone looks the same, talks the same, buys the same, and consumes the same but rather it is an eclectic and diverse community.

Bowness exists as an independent piece of geography in Calgary with the Transcanada highway, the Bow River and two bridges at either end providing clear territorial markers. For most Calgarians there are no reasons to drive through Bowness: it is not a shortcut to some destination, nor is it a neighbourhood with much to draw or attract people except for a bicycle store (Bow Cycle) and a park (Bowness Park). Yet Bowness has a strong sense of identity. The majority of the folks in this 10,000 person strong neighbourhood consider themselves Bownesians and proudly display 'I ♥ Bowness' bumper stickers or t-shirts. Amongst Calgarians, Bowness has a reputation of being a troubled and lower-class neighbourhood. Recently the Calgary Herald listed Bowness as the neighbourhood with the fourth highest number of murders in Calgary over the past twenty years so the reputation is not without some warrant.

Awaken's desire is to weave itself into the fabric of this neighbourhood and to be a community that can engage the social justice issues while also inviting others to become followers of Jesus. To this extent a number of strategic elements are part of Awaken's calling. Firstly, in order to missionally engage a neighbourhood, the people must not be your projects or conquests, but rather must be your neighbours, especially in Bowness where there is such a strong, independent identity. You cannot be an outsider, you must be part of the community and you must wear the mantle of Bownesian with pride.

Awaken is moving into the neighbourhood. My family and I purchased a half duplex where we rent out the basement and the five of us live on the top floor sharing 950 square feet, two bedrooms and one bathroom. It's cozy but it also represents what we want to be about: a simple family that relies on relationships to define us rather than stuff. After six months into this journey two other members of Awaken have purchased in Bowness and most others are looking this way when they are able to enter the market. Our own experience of living in the neighbourhood means that my oldest daughter can walk to school, we can meet and love other kids, families and people around us and we can pray and gain a sense of what God is up to in this place.

Church Planting in a post-Christendom context also means that one of your strategies must be to not adopt past methods and measures of success. It cannot be about attendance, owning a building and having a six or seven figure budget. This is what most churches are already trying to achieve or have achieved. Therefore church planting in post-Christendom recognizes that the margins are the place to call home. Instead of trying the find the best piece of real estate and attracting people through the widest array of programs, Awaken is realizing that being vulnerable is an opportunity. We are the ones without a home, without power, and without a clue, and so God can use us.

Much like Jesus sending out the 72 in Luke 10 and asking them to take nothing, to go as lambs and to rely on the hospitality of strangers, Awaken has been blessed to accept this role and the reality of God going before us. And in doing so, Awaken now has partners such as Bow Waters Community Church who have provided us with their small facility to gather on Sunday evenings and a plot of land to start a community garden and the Bowness Community Association which has invited me to be on their board to help re-establish its presence in the neighbourhood. Awaken has realized that instead of trying to carve out and claim our piece of the turf, we will best serve the neighbourhood and reach people through the relationships we build in ways beyond the four walls of a building.

Another reality of church planting in a post-Christendom era is that it requires creative approaches to ensure longevity and the commitment to the neighbourhood. I believe that becoming bi-vocational is a key strategic reality for church planters. Adopting a bi-vocational model has allowed Awaken to dream of means of blessing the neighbourhood (a 3rd space, community garden…) instead of focusing all of its finances on one salary. Moreover, we have maintained the ethos of Awaken where it isn't one full-time pastor who is paid to do everything, know everything and be everything. Awaken continues to go forward relying on everyone to help create our expression of the church.

My transition into bi-vocationality has gone quite smoothly. I am fortunate to be connected to an online software company that believes in what we are doing. This company which provides an online means of managing facilities and assets has hired me to provide client support and data management on a ¾ time basis and recognizes that I will occasionally need to have lunch or coffee with folks. This has been nothing short of a God-send and I wonder if more Christian business folks began to view their enterprises as means of supporting missional endeavors and church planting what a difference that could make. This job along with a part-time salary from Awaken allows me to stay in the neighbourhood, support my family, pay our bills, and stay committed to Bowness regardless of how Awaken's finances may fluctuate.

"On You will Go"

Having arrived in Bowness and having begun to establish relationships and make inroads into the fabric of the neighbourhood, a new question has risen in our midst. How do you stay faithful to the calling and mission God has placed upon you? This is a vital question and a question of spiritual formation. We have come to the conclusion that submitting ourselves to a covenant or rule would allow us to all share a common vision, a common mission, and common practices to ensure our faithfulness to the calling. This is our covenant in its most recent form; we call it our SENT Covenant:

S - Story

We affirm the historic and orthodox Christian faith. We believe that God has revealed himself through the Holy and Inspired Scriptures. We believe that God has invited us to be rooted in Him and His desires to bring wholeness and peace towards others, towards the earth, towards Himself and within ourselves.

Covenant: We covenant to root ourselves in the Biblical narrative.

E - Eat

We affirm the necessity of practices that provide us with the eyes to see and the ears to hear God in the everyday moments of our lives. We believe in engaging in spiritual disciplines that allow us to see, listen, taste and touch the reality of God and that prompt us to remain faithful to the path God has called us to.

Covenant: We covenant to engage in spiritual practices that keep us focused on our journey to be conformed to the image of Jesus. (eat, pray, tithe, solitude, art, writing, exercise…)

N - Neighbourhood

We affirm our role, as God's people, to serve and bless others. The Church as the body of Jesus is to follow His example and share his heart for others in our broken and fragmented world. We believe in following Jesus towards those who are suffering and facing injustice and living out the redemptive and transformative message of hope that is found in Jesus.

Covenant: We covenant to love and serve others in our neighbourhoods.

T - Together

We affirm that everyone bears God's image. Through sharing in each other's sufferings and celebrations, loving and forgiving one another, we can journey forward. We were made for community and within loving relationships, God's truth takes on flesh and blood, and we are not alone. We believe that together through Jesus we can become more than we our by ourselves.

Covenant: We covenant to pursue God together in community

Another aspect of spiritual formation for Awaken is observing the Christian calendar. Our Sunday gatherings are opportunities for us to eat, worship, share, receive teaching and focus ourselves around the major moments in Jesus' life. To do this, Awaken has created a calendar that guides us on eight journeys each year. Each journey is led by a team of people at Awaken and involves cultivating an environment where we can learn and experience together the theme or movement of that particular journey. (See illustration A).

Illustration A

The diagram is a circular calendar wheel with the months arranged around the outside: January, February, March, April, May, June, July, August, September, October, November, December. Inside the wheel are labels: Advent; Uniting the Tribes: Community-Wide Focus:; Inductive/Exegetical Biblical Journey; Lent; Awaken Covenant; Living in light of the resurrection:; Summer Spiritual Journey; Gospel – Centred.

Finally, a vital piece to our spiritual formation and our mission in Bowness is our small groups. Awaken currently has five small groups that gather together throughout the week. The groups are small (four to seven) and exist to provide a sense of community and a sense of mission together. The small groups corporately hold to the SENT covenant and as a result the small groups can discern which practices will best suit them, and what aspect of justice, compassion, environmental stewardship, or service they can provide to Bowness. We are just in the process of launching these small groups and for many of us, it is the first time we will have submitted to a covenant or rule that binds us all together. We are praying that instead of being viewed as restricting and limiting, we will see that the covenant provides the centre from which we can all launch and pursue God as He brings wholeness to ourselves, our neighbours and the Earth.

"Your Mountain is Waiting"

I think I've shared enough of our vision and what we believe God has called us to. Let me end with a story. When I was a child, Christmas morning was a big deal. I lived in a home that was fortunate enough to have Santa Claus come visit every year and bring awesome gifts and presents. The year of my 10th Christmas I was anxiously looking forward to a new remote controlled car that I had been asking and petitioning for.

I lived in a cul-de-sac that didn't have much traffic and I could already imagine how I would steer the car around different obstacles and materials that lay outside my front door.

Christmas Eve arrived but the trouble was, I couldn't sleep, or at least I didn't sleep for long. Sometime in the middle of the night I awoke with excitement and anticipation. The house was dark and quiet, yet I was awake and alert and I quietly crept down the stairs to see if my wishes had come true. And there before my eyes were three stockings and three piles of gifts laid out, one for my sister, my brother and my self.

The first thing I noticed was this large remote controlled monster truck and I went right for it. I picked up the large box and began to drool over the new found possibilities of having a monster truck instead of just a car. Yet as I begin to look through the stocking and the other gifts in that pile, I saw that this was not for me, but rather this was my little brother's gift from Santa. So I quickly turned to the other stocking and pile of gifts and I saw another remote controlled vehicle. This time it was a van…

A van…. In my pile from Santa was a little remote controlled van. What was Santa thinking? How could my five-year-old brother get the monster truck, and I get the small van? So I looked around and made the switch. I reasoned that Santa surely must have made a mistake, and that since I was the older brother, I clearly should be the one with the larger remote controlled vehicle, and surely not a van!

I snuck back into my room, closed the door and tried to go back to sleep but I couldn't. Eventually the sun began to rise and I ventured out of my room. I had done some thinking and realized that there is no way Santa could make a mistake and that either my brother behaved like an angel and deserved the monster truck, or I had been a brat and was punished with the van: either way I decided to accept the reality and I hustled down the stairs to switch back the gifts. I had just made the switch back when the rest of the family entered the room. There were smiles and cries of excitement from everyone, especially from my brother when he saw his truck. I pretended like I was surprised and pleased with what Santa had brought me, but all the time I was watching my brother and his truck and had gently set my van down, still in its box, to the side.

Fresh

My father noticed this and came over and grabbed the van and sat down with me to open it. He noticed the way I was watching my brother and the monster truck and told me to watch closely. As I watched, I noticed something about the monster truck: it was large, but it was meant for a little child. The control was not remote, but rather the cord was attached permanently to the truck. It couldn't go fast or do any cool tricks. All you could do was walk behind and steer it as in crawled along in a small, simple way. Meanwhile my Dad had taken the van out of its packaging and I realized that this was the true remote controlled vehicle. Although I was not envisioning a van, it more than accomplished what I hoped the remote controlled vehicle would. It would race around our cul-de-sac and through the courses I had set up at incredible speeds. It was the vehicle I was meant to have and I realized that Santa had got it right all along.

Awaken's story is our story. It is the dream my family and I and our amazing little community is meant to live out. God has always got it right; we just have to not be afraid and believe. We traded in the large monster truck for our little remote controlled van when we walked out of the large established church and moved into Bowness.

Now as a fluid little group, empowered by the Holy Spirit and moved by the heart beat of our Savior, we finally get to run through the course designed for us. It is the path least taken, but it is one we walk together. There are still plenty of obstacles. We are still trying to figure out what leadership looks like, friends we thought would continue with us have stepped away, and we are still learning to love. But we are free to go as the Wind blows, dream dreams that we never thought possible, and keep asking questions to prompt us to faithfulness. Soon a community garden will exists in Bowness, a possible coffee shop or 3rd space will be coming down the road and Lord willing folks who are struggling will experience the grace and mercy of our Lord Jesus. To Him be the Glory.

* All internal titles are provided by "Oh, The Places You'll Go" by Dr. Seuss (Yep, I'm a father of three and he is our theologian of choice lately!)

Phil Harbridge

Phil Harbridge was a youth pastor for twenty-five years and is currently teaching Biblical Studies and Faith & Culture at Richmond Christian Secondary School in Richmond B.C. Phil received his Bachelor of Arts degree in History (and Minor in Communications) from Crown College, Minnesota. Following that, Phil completed his Master of Divinity at Denver Seminary, Colorado. Phil has pastored in Denver, Kitchener/Waterloo, and Vancouver. Most recently he completed his Doctor of Ministry from Carey Theological College. "Dr. Phil" is an avid runner, marathoner, and triathlete. He and his wife Kay have two (grown) daughters. Phil's website is http://philharbridge.com and Breathe is found at www.breatheonline.org.

Breathe

– Phil Harbridge

My wife and I and our two daughters have lived in Richmond since 1992, and in our current home in the Seafair area of Richmond since 1999. The City of Richmond website describes the city as:

> ...a culturally diverse and geographically unique community centrally located on Canada's west coast, in Greater Vancouver, 20 minutes from downtown Vancouver, and 25 minutes from the US border. With a population of over 181,942 people, Richmond is a growing dynamic urban centre with a unique mix of residential and commercial property, agricultural lands, industrial parks, waterways and natural areas...Much of the recent population growth has been made up of Asian immigrants. People of Chinese or South Asian ancestry now represent nearly sixty per cent of Richmond residents.[50]

Fortunately, many people in the greater Vancouver area (Vancouver, Richmond, Surrey, White Rock, New Westminster, Burnaby,) easily move between cities for work, worship, and recreation. This means that any church or faith community can be considered accessible regardless of one's suburb of residence. According to the Yellow Pages, there are currently sixty-nine religious groups or churches in Richmond that meet on a regular basis.[51]

---

50   http://www.richmond.ca/home.htm
51   http://www.yellow.ca/bl/f.jsp

Fresh

BREATHE Christian Society formed and began "breathing" in October of 2004 as an independent and informal family meeting in my home in Richmond, B.C. It was a simple and rudimentary beginning to a spiritual community. BREATHE was not a church plant, nor a denominationally-financed outpost. Instead, it was a gathering of family and friends with no budget, an ambiguous vision, and yet the certainty that we were doing the right thing in the right place.

In recent decades the church has learned again to deal in experiences – to focus on weaving together the daily experiences of life with an every day faith. Faith communities are committed to offering spiritual fragments to those who are on a quest and rethinking their beliefs. As these people begin constructing a theology of their own, fragments of the Christian narrative are often used. As Steve Taylor indicates:

> Many people today are spiritual tourists—willing to stroll the pick-and-mix supermarket of spiritual options, looking for spiritual practises. They search out ritual and mystery, hoping for relevance and cultural coherence. They want an individualism holistically connected with others.[52]

Spirituality is "in the air" (just Google "spirituality" and read any of the 80 million hits). For centuries, God's people have toured or made journeys: from Abraham's sojourn into Canaan to Israel's wilderness wanderings, from the Via Dolorosa to Paul's missionary journeys, from medieval pilgrimages to the literary imagery of John Bunyan's writings. But as each of these examples proves, the journey is rarely linear. Our journey is to encounter the living God, the God who really exists. The question is: what will take us there? What will help us on that journey?

After transitioning out of a rewarding and complex ministry in a large traditional urban church, our family felt unmotivated to re-enter another traditional church community. Trading one church for another was not at the top of our list of priorities; however, encountering God in a fresh and mysterious way, was. Fortunately, after resigning from our previous

---

52   Steve Taylor, *The Out of Bounds Church? Learning to Create a Community of Faith in a Culture of Change* (Grand Rapids, Mich.: Zondervan Publishing, 2005), 81.

church and moving past some of the bittersweet events of the final weeks, our daughters still wanted God and shared worship experiences. Many years had been invested with families and young people in our former church and God had blessed us with rich relationships and fruitful ministry.

Although our spirits were buoyant toward God, we also felt needy as a family. We had become weary of regularly giving, serving, and supporting others in their spiritual maturation sometimes at the expense of our own. The political landscape in our previous church and the routine of predictable worship had taken its toll. We believed that there was so much more, so much deeper life and richer worship experiences that God had in store for us. Our family was primed and craving a breath of fresh air from God.

Instead of frantically readying ourselves to venture out in search of a church building, we felt compelled to simply show up in our own living room and invite God to meet with us. We did not want to be distracted with style, or fashion, or appearances, or image, or carpet or anything else that has so often marred the focus of church-goers. Our first gatherings in the fall of 2004 were marked by simplicity, intimacy, and honesty. We were a family, and we were worshipping. We sought to weave together what we believed with how we behaved, to worship and experience God in real life, in a place where we most often live life.

As creatively as possible we sought to encounter God and experience his character. Group and personal readings, lighting candles of presence, singing and listening to music, silence, delicious brunch, and lively dialogue all filled our first breaths. No two weeks were ever the same, though every week God's Spirit led us into deeper communion and appreciation of Jesus. Occasionally the dogs would interrupt us or we'd laugh at the meandering conversation, but it felt natural, and it made sense to be at home, with God.

A few friends who had heard that we were setting aside time on Sunday mornings to focus on God started to join in on the humble gatherings. As a family we had not looked to grow anything. God seemed to be showing up in our small worship gatherings and that was deeply satisfying and enriching. Honest, authentic God-seekers were becoming curious, then interested, and eventually committed to setting aside time each week to be together with God.

For several weeks this nondescript, fragile, needy community drew together around God without any thought of ecclesiological structure. Some people explored the group for a time and moved on, while others found a home. It was suggested by one of the participants that perhaps we try to organize ourselves without compromising the spontaneity and flexibility of our worship. Given the size of the group and our affirmation of shared leadership, structure seemed irrelevant except for the value of accountability, decision-making, growing awareness, and potentially charitable status.

In January of 2005, after agreeing that the name BREATHE characterized the desire of our community to fill our lungs and life with God, a skilled young lawyer from the group filled out the government applications to formally organize and register our community as a church. By February 2005, BREATHE Christian Society was formed as an incorporated Society in the province of British Columbia, and two months later became a federal charitable organization.

From first breath to formally recognized church community, the focus has never strayed from breathing in God's Spirit and life, encountering the Divine, and supporting each other on the journey. The mission of BREATHE, from the community website, states: "As people created for community, and through our dependence on the living God, we seek to inspire the imagination, refresh the soul, and nurture the body, all within the context of deep, interdependent relationships."

The process of emerging has never stopped. In the spring of 2005, BREATHE launched a website designed to connect, inform, and inspire people from all walks of life. This too has continued to take shape and evolve. Many people near and far have made use of the online chat rooms, message boards, photo galleries, information pages, Pay Pal method of contributing or tithing, prayer posts, and attractive communication in order to be supported, give support, or simply find out how to connect with BREATHE.

As a small home-based faith community, it is our conviction that all that we are and do is to be a compliment to God. Our worship is not just for a few hours on Sunday and perhaps the occasional Wednesday night. All of our days, decisions and hopes, our lively conversations and humdrum Tuesday afternoons, *everything*, is an expression of worship: we want to live with a sense of the eternal. Whenever we gather together or are on our own, we know that there is a whole lot more going on than we realize.

In light of that, when we set aside time to appreciate and give God the highest compliment, we have seen it as a continuation of our daily lives—our eating, and laughing, thinking, talking, singing, dancing, watching, praying, greeting, walking, wondering, stillness, garbage-gathering, serving, contributing, reading. Everything we do is an expression of thoughtful gratitude. We believe, as Neil Cole states, that "church should happen wherever life happens. You shouldn't have to leave life to go to church."[53]

When the home-based faith community gathers for Inhale, the Sunday morning worship experience, there is a sense of freedom and comfort that evokes honesty and authenticity with each other and God. Congregating in a home has the feel of a house party, celebration, or a large Thanksgiving family meal. On these occasions and in this environment, those who gather as the BREATHE community openly and willingly talk about their daily experiences and share the stories of their lives. It is our sense that worship is about noticing what God is doing in each others' lives. When we appreciate the involvement that God has in our lives personally and corporately, our thoughtfulness becomes thankfulness and finally a narrative of worship.

It is our conviction, along with Herbert Anderson and Edward Foley, that:

> Like other human rituals, worship is neither just an exercise in divine data distribution nor a rehearsal of celestial rules. Rather, public worship is a significant, even indispensable way for

---

53   Neil Cole, *Organic Church* (San Francisco, CA: Jossey-Bass, 2005) 24.

believers to exercise and acquire faith. It is a way in which believers discover how God is or can be a part of their lives. Worship is also an important medium for discovering the significance that belief in God has for the way one shapes personal relationships or conducts worldly affairs. Worship is a critical exercise in meaning making for believers...public worship cannot enable the human-divine encounter without adequate attention to narrative. In particular, sacred rituals must respect and balance human stories – both individual and communal – with the divine narrative without manipulation or deceit.[54]

As we gather over a creatively tasty brunch, sitting and standing in the living/dining room, we talk and we tell the stories of our lives. Eventually the group will make its way to the family room that is comfortably furnished and decorated. Here, we continue our talking and worship as one of us (usually myself) facilitates various spiritual practices. Because we value flexibility, what may be planned and what actually happens can look quite different. Interruptions are welcome if God is directing the experience.

Usually we will have a time of silence in order to slow down, reflect on the scriptural command to, "Be still and know that I am God" (Isaiah 46:10), and to practice listening. Images and music may accompany the stillness or perhaps nothing but the rhythm of our breathing can be heard. The atmosphere is always very relaxed – regular coffee refills abound – though earnest in devotion. The BREATHE community enjoys worshipping through such practices as listening to music, singing, going for walks along the western dyke of Richmond, discussing teaching and music videos, reading and thinking about Scripture, watching movies, drawing, painting, writing, consuming and remembering by means of the Eucharist, telling our stories and praying.

Although the worship, intimate community, and spiritual nurture have resonated with those who draw together, many questions have continued to capture my attention, especially as I explore the spiritual formation

---

54   Herbert Anderson and Edward Foley, *Mighty Stories, Dangerous Rituals: Weaving Together the Human and the Divine* (San Francisco: Jossey-Bass, 1998), 42-43.

practices of other nascent faith communities. Are people actually growing in their spiritual lives? Do the burgeoning community and the communal experiences afford people the opportunity for spiritual growth? Do our spiritual practices nurture spiritual formation? All of those questions were in the back of my mind as we continued to meet, grow, and weave together our spiritual and practical lives.

This study is the result of those questions, the desire to be changed by our experiences with the Divine, and the journey that we are privileged to travel with God. It is not our desire to have a form of godliness (ritual, spiritual practices) while ignoring or denying the power (God's transforming presence). BREATHE's fundamental conviction is that God is to be experienced and we are to be changed by that experience. Or as Hebrews 11:6 states, "But without faith no one can please God. We must believe that God is real and that he rewards everyone who searches for him" (CEV).

The Gospel and Culture

Breathing is essential and basic to human growth. And spiritual growth is no different. For the BREATHE community, this means "inhaling" (communal worship) and "exhaling" (intersecting culture and faith). While Inhale generally involves an opportunity to appreciate life and God, Exhale is an open invitation to connect ones worldview, ideas, culture and wonder in a familiar setting – the Pub. Every other Tuesday night, some of the BREATHE community gather at the Elephant & Castle Restaurant & Pub in their "upper room" known as The Sandbar, to relax, nourish our physical appetite with good food and beverages, and to examine our world, faith, and lives. Exhale is held in a culturally popular setting and often attracts more spiritual seekers than followers of Jesus. From time to time, even patrons and employees of the Pub will join in on the conversation and share their stories.

"I enjoy coming to these Tuesday nights, you all disagree so agreeably," commented Wade, a regular at Exhale. The opportunity to take an hour or two after a long day and simply unwind, all the while getting your thoughts and honest feelings out and perhaps understand a bit more about social issues, society, faith, etc. has clearly resonated with many. The drop-in nature of Exhale means that no one is sure who will be there from week to week, but the discussions, if not informative and enlightening, are always personal and...cathartic. Our BREATHE community has become very close to many of the staff and management at the Elephant and Castle, and from the hugs, waves and smiles, it's evident that we look forward to seeing each other on Tuesday.

"I have nowhere else in my life where I'm able to spend some time like this with such a variety of people to discuss life," revealed Ian who struggles to get to Exhale due to work but who passionately and desperately enjoys the gathering. In a sense, Exhale offers a place to be yourself and gain some perspective. That is something we have found is lacking in our culture. From Vancouver to Burnaby to White Rock and Surrey, people come by bus, car and bike as often as their schedule will allow them. Exhale is not an attempt to be cool and alternative (whatever that means). We just enjoy being ourselves together and welcoming new conversation partners.

Connecting our faith and culture is not limited to the engaging gatherings on Tuesday nights at Exhale. In fact, culturally redemptive experiences occur frequently as each person from the community lives his or her faith however strong or struggling it may be. From seemingly benign conversations at Starbucks to dialogue over a Saturday morning run, the line between culture and Christianity is erased. God becomes part of the fabric of our everyday lives. Our best intentions on Sundays as we Inhale are to love God. "In loving me you made me loving," asserted Augustine, and for the BREATHE community, that love is experienced through some common practices.

Common Meal

The emerging faith community of BREATHE regularly experiences hospitality in the form of the common meal. Our worship incorporates eating in community and celebrating the goodness and faithfulness of God. The common meal as we practice it comes in two forms: Brunch – a diverse and delicious, cold and hot, help-yourself meal that replaces breakfast and lunch and is not only amazingly tasty but healthy as well; and Communion/Eucharist – taking and eating food and drink that is intended to remind participants of the broken and bleeding body of Jesus.

It is our belief that all our eating and drinking can remind us of our finiteness and Christ's sacrifice on our behalf. At times, however, it is helpful and necessary to set apart a specific experience in order to better focus our attention. Brunch happens every week, while Communion/Eucharist may happen once a month or once every six to eight weeks.

Eating and experiencing hospitality in this way is an expression of community and unity. As Christians, our theological basis for hospitality is creation. Creation is the ultimate expression of God's hospitality to his creatures.

God's creation gives us a model for making and sharing homes with people, but the reality of God's Trinitarian life suggests that Christian hospitality goes further than that. We are not meant simply to invite people into our homes, but also to invite them into our lives. Having guests and visitors, if we do it right, is not an imposition, because we are not meant to rearrange our lives for our guests – we are meant to invite our guests to enter into our lives as they are. It is this forging of relationships that transforms entertaining (i.e., deadly dull cocktail parties at the country club) into hospitality (i.e., a simple pizza on my floor).[55]

Teacher, author and Biblical Hebrew scholar, Douglas A. Wheeler, states:

> The manner in which the first-century Christians shared their meals was part of a rich Jewish cultural tradition that has by and large been lost to modern Christianity. The first believers celebrated mealtime in the tradition of Bircath Hamazon (called "benching"), a time for family celebration, fellowship, and worship around the table that had come to be seen as an altar. The early believers not only knew, but also applied the Biblical truth that "man does not live by bread alone, but by every word that travels out of the mouth of the Lord" (Deuteronomy 8:3)…Mealtime was a time when something spiritual, something

---

55 Lauren F. Winner, *Mudhouse Sabbath* (Brewster, Mass.: Paraclette Press, 2003), 46 – 47.

special was produced. It was also a time when people talked about their day, their experiences, their work, their struggles…what makes them laugh. Basically as we eat and talk with and to each other we share not only the food that God provides (bringing a realization that we are dependent on Him) but also our very lives.[56]

Implicatory Dialogue

The notion of dialogue is not foreign to spiritual groups or worshippers. Over the centuries, the social, dynamic, and theological process of dialoging about faith, truth, and life has been commonplace, both formally and informally. The perspective of implication over application, however, is an experience that is being rejuvenated by Doug Pagitt, Pastor of Solomon's Porch in Minneapolis, Minnesota.

There is a fine yet significant difference between application—the buzzword of the past century, and implication – the intuitive meta-narrative from outside time. Application is about how a piece of information fits into your life. Implication is not about fitting; it's about redefining. It's not a value-added suggestion; it's a call to see the story and join in it…[57]

Progressive implicatory dialogue is where the content of the presentation is established in the context of a healthy relationship between the presenter and the listeners, and substantive changes in the content are then created as a result of this relationship.

The ability to take a nugget of truth (information) from Scripture and rub it on our lives in such a way that we utilize it, has been a priority in preaching and churches for many years. For followers of Jesus it has become our default mode of making Scripture practical. The essential disconnect with this form of integration is that it is individualistic and usually judgmental. The question in application usually rests on me, on I:

---

56   http://www.restorationfoundation.org/volume%2010/43_28.htm.

57   Doug Pagitt, *Preaching Re-Imagined: The Role of the Sermon in Communities of Faith* (Grand Rapids, Mich.: Zondervan, 2003), 97, 102.

"Do you see what I see?" or "Do you know what I know?" And this process is reinforced by a preacher or leader who seeks to make that application to everyone in earshot regardless of the diversity we possess as people. Application has a sense of *me* to it; implication has a sense of *us*. As Doug Pagitt explains:

> This difference is crucial to the ways in which we understand ourselves as God's people. Application allows us to remain disconnected, to think of our faith in individualistic terms. But nowhere in the Bible do we see faith as an individual endeavor. It is always a communal practice. Even the stories about people of faith – Moses, David, Job – are told from a communal perspective; the point is never what happens to them but what happens because of them. The sense of us that comes through implication opens our communities to the notion that we aren't simply people who gather once a week for a common experience, but we are part of something bigger than ourselves. Suddenly, we tap into the power of the community to be a source of formation, of life change ... Think about the ways in which the disciples responded whenever they listened to Jesus preach. They wondered what this call would mean for them. They talked to each other about what they'd heard. They asked Jesus questions about how his words were changing them. They were not asking questions of application, but of reorientation.[58]

It would be tempting to think of implicatory dialogue as simply discussion. However, as mentioned above, while implicatory dialogue may appear discussion-like, the content or perspective is uniquely different. Implicatory dialogue is talking about God's life in us as a community.

During Inhale, our conversation and interaction is a time where the community is implicated by the story of God, becoming part of it and arranging their lives around it. The content for these discussions, for this

---

58   Ibid., 99-100.

study, came from the weekly use of the Nooma[59] video series (numbers 1-5, 7, 8,10,11).

Contemplative Prayer

The BREATHE community seeks to practice contemplative prayer in order to be fully present or "at home" with God. Thomas Green speaks about the experience of contemplative prayer and says:

> There is a newfound joy simply in being still in the presence of the Lord, just as good friends find joy simply in being together. They are not self-conscious or nervous about silences. They don't plan their conversation or analyze their relationship. They don't really "think about" each other much when they are together. They just are, and they are happy to be together, whatever may be happening. Talking and silence are spontaneous and easy and relaxed – not laboured or artificial.[60]

Each week the BREATHE community engages in a particular aspect of contemplative prayer from the following:

1. Intercessory prayer – prayers made on behalf of someone else.

2. Body prayer – using body posture and physical actions to connect with God and communicate desire.

3. Prayer walking – talking to God while walking in his creation.

---

59   http://www.nooma.com We can get anything we want, from anywhere in the world, whenever we want it. That's how it is and that's how we want it to be. Still, our lives aren't any different than other generations before us. Our time is. We want spiritual direction, but it has to be real for us and available when we need it. We want a new format for getting Christian perspectives. NOOMA is the new format. It's short films with communicators that really speak to us. Compact, portable, and concise. Each NOOMA touches on issues that we care about, that we want to talk about, and it comes in a way that fits our world. It's a format that's there for us when we need it, as we need it, how we need it.

60   Thomas H. Green, S.J. *When the Well Runs Dry: Prayer Beyond the Beginnings* (Notre Dame, Indiana: Ave Maria Press, 1998), 51.

4. Silence and Solitude – being still and quiet in God's presence in order to listen.

Creative Arts

When we consciously attend to an object, especially an art object, we will have some kind of reaction to it. The response may be subtle or it may be strong; we may be turned off, aroused, repulsed, delighted, or disappointed; we may be moved to tears, frightened, bored, or baffled. But no matter how we respond, we are different for having had the viewing, or the hearing – for having paid attention. Our memories, even our ideas, are essentially constructed out of images and colours, spatial relationships, smells, sensations, and sounds, more than they are made of words ordered into sentences – even when we record and transmit them this way.

Therefore, for the arts to be an effective worship experience, we must give up the familiarity of the status quo (whether comforting or stifling) and take a chance on the unknown.[61] To risk the gaze into the creative unknown is to not only encounter the very nature of God (creative Creator), but to realize that the thing we see is not the truth itself but a means for our encounter with the Truth. "All of us, with unveiled faces, seeing the glory of the Lord as though reflected in a mirror, are being transformed into the same image from one degree of glory to another; for this comes from the Lord, the Spirit" (2 Corinthians 3:18). Each week during Inhale, we engage in a particular aspect of the creative arts from among the following:

1. Music and Technology – facilitating singing and thought by using visual PowerPoint slides together with pre-recorded music from various genres.

2. Writing – creating written expressions of worship through prayers, poems, letters, songs, thoughts about God.

---

61   Robin M. Jensen, *The Substance of Things Seen: Art, Faith, and the Christian Community* (Grand Rapids, Mich.: William B. Eerdmans Publishing, 2004), 3.

3. Drawing and Painting – creating visual expressions of worship through sketching or Buddha Board paintings.

Common Practices

"In many ways," states Oliver Davies, "Christianity lives by its ability to rediscover its past," and Davies goes on to say:

> The history of Christianity shows a constant tendency toward invigorating revival and rediscovery of its roots as well as to polemics surrounding the varying definitions of tradition. The way to appropriate traditions from the past, originally practised in social and spiritual contexts very different from our own, is problematic.[62]

Our faith is a historically rich and culturally diverse faith that has gone through vast changes and cycles of experience and renewal. Nevertheless, one value of studying the practices of early faith communities is that they alert us to possibilities of Christian existence and formation which are both ancient and new.

The spiritual formation practices of the BREATHE community are rooted in history. As I have discussed above, from the early church notions of community, home-based gathering, and participatory style to the Benedictine and Celtic practices of prayer, *lectio*, silence, hospitality, and poetry, there is a thread of connection to our current spiritual community.

Although the specific form of spiritual practice does not mirror the historic form exactly, the connection is clear. Benedictine and Celtic Christians gathered in monasteries or circular walled villages in order to devote themselves to encountering and serving God. Their gatherings included everyday life experiences – eating, talking, thinking, and working.

From these ancient roots arise the BREATHE practices of the common meal and implicatory dialogue. The quest for the Divine caused early

---

62   Davies, 24-25.

Christians to engage in various forms of meditation, contemplation, and prayer as well as reading and writing about Scripture. The BREATHE practices of contemplative prayer and the creative arts are linked. The rich heritage of ancient practices of spiritual formation has enriched and renewed the BREATHE community in the 21st century.

Re:Fresh

Re:Fresh

New Life From Old Roots

Jim Loepp Thiessen

Jim Loepp Thiessen has been in full-time ministry for seventeen years, twelve of those in a traditional rural church outside of Baden, Ontario. He spent almost two years teaching about the missional church with his denomination, Mennonite Church Canada. He loves to cook, tease his three children, read, and tell flying stories about the days when he had a pilot's licence. He is married to Ingrid, who is also a pastor. The Gathering is located online here: www.thegatheringsite.ca/about.html.

The Gathering Church Story

– Jim Loepp Thiessen

My name is Jim Thiessen and I pastor The Gathering along with my wife Ingrid. Like many others, I had no real desire to plant a church – but God had different ideas.

Our family recently watched "Quest for the Bay," the story of eight people who recreated the York boat journey from Winnipeg to the Hudson Bay in the mid 1840's. We watched them continually repair the large wooden boat, damaged from the rocks underneath the rapids, and portage, with long ropes, the one ton vessel thirty-four times, including once over a kilometre portage which took a week. And all this carrying two hundred pound packs, eating a diet of lard and blueberries, dealing with relentless swarms of bugs, and finally crashing the boat in the middle of some rapids. I said to my wife, "Every church planter should watch this video."

Church planting was dropped in my lap. I pastored a one hundred and sixty year old church for over twelve years on a country road outside of Baden, Ontario. It was ministry that felt for the most part like being on a large ship: lots of momentum, slow and lumbering most of the time, making turns slowly and carefully. Gradually, during my tenure at that congregation, I felt like my heart was being prepared for something new – a risky adventure. Opportunities to candidate in other churches in our Mennonite denomination didn't feel like options for me: it felt like more of the same.

During the time when I was discerning next steps, four or five people asked me over the course of about a month, "Have you ever thought about church planting?" I had, but put the thought out of my mind. I knew however that I had a real heart for those outside the church. Through my experience of running the Alpha program, I realized how much I cared about folks from outside the church who were asking questions about God and faith.

In a period of deep questioning about next steps in my ministry, and having a bad day where I felt desperate to hear God, I drove over a hill on the west side of Kitchener, where I saw a sign for a new subdivision which said, "Welcome to Crossroads, your new beginning."

On that day, it felt somehow like God was speaking to me through that sign. I wanted to ignore it, but the nudge to explore this church planting venture wouldn't go away. I spoke with someone from Outreach Canada about church planting, but after that conversation, felt, with some relief, that I was more into revitalization than planting. On a day when another job within the larger church loomed as a possibility, it felt clear to me, however, that I was being invited by the Spirit of God to start a new church.

As I took a few tentative steps towards starting a new church, doors started to open, and things started to come together. It scared me silly. My biggest fear, apart from hearing statistics like that two out of three church plants don't work was, *Will we be able to pull this off financially?* and *What if we fail?*

I didn't know how we would build this church: I'd never done anything like this before. It would have to be Jesus doing the building. Alpha had worked well for us in the past, and I knew that we would do that again as one piece of our community connection. I was certain it had to be about serving others, but I didn't have much of a blueprint. Setting one-year numerical goals had never fit with me, hard as I tried, and I didn't believe in that style of planning in any case. I had done teaching on the missional church with my denomination, and had read extensively about the church and mission, but in the end, it was, *Okay, so what are we going to do?*

We found a few things that were compelling. We would celebrate with our community; we would serve them in love; we would gather in small groups as a church; we would try and make our worship "post Christendom" in its approach. That is, we would not start with the assumption in our worship that you knew the gospel story, you just weren't telling us.

I also knew it had to start with Jesus, not Menno Simons, the sixteenth century leader of the Anabaptists of which I was a part. It needed to be about going beyond the cultural values embedded in my Anabaptist tradition to meeting people at the level of "transcultural" values. For example, rather than inviting folks to serve because that's what Mennonites do, it would mean service as a way of embracing and loving others and as a way of following Jesus.

I knew from the start that we were being called to do this plant within our denomination. Our denomination, a collection of about ninety Mennonite churches in Eastern Canada, had not done much church planting, but the new mission minister was very enthusiastic about the possibility. In fact, he saw church planting as one of his key emphases, and had himself planted churches! His personal support from the outset was critical in making this happen. One of the best things my denomination has done, apart from our mission minister support, is freeing me from huge growth pressure. They didn't come with, "We need to be this size by this time..."

When the Yorkmen took sixteen days to travel up lake Winnipeg, a trip that two hundred years ago used to take only nine days, the modern day Yorkmen weren't discouraged, but celebrated the first major step. Our denomination worked with us in a similar way. I thought, *We aren't growing really fast, but we are growing.* They celebrated what we were doing, and what God was doing among us. They recognized we were different, (our worship is more "contemporary," rather than traditional like many churches in the larger fold), and they were able to work with that difference. They love hearing the stories of what is happening among us.

For every step that I took to begin, God seemed to open a door. I spent a year working part-time in an interim ministry while we assembled a team of folks to walk with this new venture. After a year of prayer, visioning, and a few connecting events with the community we felt called to serve, the community I had encountered with the "Crossroads" sign, "The Gathering Church" began meeting on Sunday evenings. The dream of a voyage to the Bay was becoming a reality!

On the night of our launch, one of the folks from the community who came decided she needed to recommit her life to Jesus after walking away from her faith as a teenager. I was completely unprepared for that response on an opening night! I had prayed for that kind of encounter in my previous ministry, and it never happened. It served as a sign from God for me, that God was somehow in this new ministry. The response of this community person, based on what I said, also showed me that it was God doing the calling, not me. I hadn't even invited people to consider following Jesus on our opening night of worship.

I didn't have a huge theological grid on which to hang this new venture. As an Anabaptist, I placed a high value on service to others, and that I needed to do this without starting a war. My internal sensibilities were clearly to function more as "quiet in the land," meaning to serve others quietly, but don't express what it's all about. I believed that if it was "the God of peace that crushed Satan under our feet," then there was something about blessing, serving, and bringing peace to others that brought the blessing of God to others.

When we went through the community asking people why they thought most people didn't go to church, "no time, too boring..." were high on the list. I knew a traditional-style worship service would not, for the most part, engage others who were seeking. I knew our worship would need to use media because we lived in a media-driven, visual culture. Providentially, God brought people who were able to bring that vision to reality. More than that, I needed to create a space where we were sensitive to visitors, not overwhelming them with church culture. We needed to create a hospitable space where visitors felt like it was their party, or at least created for them.

I believed with my heart and soul that Jesus was going ahead of us (Luke 10) no matter what happened, and that the missional task was to pay attention to where God was moving, always.

Everything I read about church planting said it was not going to be easy. One fellow planter, a few years ahead of me said, "You're in for a real ride." I read Steve Sjogren's book on planting, he said, "don't even attempt church planting unless you are ready to have your motives torn apart by God…" That was scary to me. Like the people in the York boat, swarmed by mosquitoes, and dealing with wet equipment because of a leaky boat, I asked again and again why I was doing this.

Yet I also knew that this was a step of faithfulness. I knew from my reading about church planting that, like travelling to the Hudson Bay, it was going to be very discouraging at times. I decided early on in the venture to adopt the Biblical metaphor of "manna." That is, I always tried to see where God was providing, and being revealed on a daily basis, rather than looking for massive manifestations of God's presence.

Indeed, there was and is always something for which to give thanks: always the "manna" is present. On a Sunday where the worship felt like it hit bottom, several volunteers came on board. Although the school we met in consistently said no to a storage spot for our equipment, after six months of prayer, they said yes. I took that yes as a sign of God's favour on our work. There were many smaller signs along the way, and I pleaded with God for eyes to see where he was moving.

To engage our community, we did tons of free stuff. We have done free car washes, hot dog give-aways, free neighbourhood parties, free raking, and on it goes. This past summer we had a one hour games event each Tuesday evening through the summer with area kids. We had between forty and sixty kids out each week for that event. While our young adults played games, I had conversation with their parents on the sidelines. They were the most amazing conversations where I learned again how far from "Christendom" those outside the church are. "So, does the government support this program…?" "No, it's actually private donations…" Several of those kids now come out for our youth events.

Slowly, service to the community has built trust in our church and this is critical. Building trust is a much larger issue than I would have guessed when we started. The adventure of lugging equipment, and doing community events to get us out there, like the Yorkmen, brought us together as a team. The best event we have done is a free community pancake breakfast on Thanksgiving Sunday. I mean "best" because one of our values apart from serving is meaningful conversation. In conversation we enter the world of those different from us. We have had people check out our church as a result of that event, because we had the time to talk with them over breakfast.

This kind of outreach has been one level of engagement. Outreach events make us feel good as a church body, they are great team building events, and they help build trust in our church. But I think we are called to go deeper, dealing with larger justice issues. I also think that when people become truly engaged, we will be renamed "The Scattering Church," because we always seem to ask God to bring people to us, when the whole New Testament emphasis is us going to them.

As a leader, I believe that my next key task is a greater focus on equipping others for the mission God has given to each of them. I also know that I have to lead with my own life by being one of the "scattered ones." For this reason I pray continually the prayer from Acts 4 for boldness in my ministry. Honestly, if there was one thing I wish for, it's simply boldness: to risk, to respond to the nudging of the Spirit, to be increasingly more creative in what we do, and to "think outside the box" in everything we do.

Some of the best times in my ministry have been where the Spirit of God has been present to bring healing to others. As I read the gospels, I notice the healing ministry of Jesus particularly efficacious with those on the fringes. God seemed to "show up" in those places in unique ways. One couple who had moved here from China took Alpha, and a month after we prayed for them to have a child they came to church thrilled because they were pregnant! I noticed the efficacy of our prayers, especially with those on the fringes of faith. The "discussion" about the reality of Jesus never happened for this couple because they experienced this answer to prayer.

We had several stories like that happening: we prayed, and God "showed up." We saw people with little or no experience of God praying, and having God show up dramatically in their lives. Take Jay, a guy addicted to heroin and crystal meth, struggling to break out of his addiction. He came into our worship service after dropping off his girlfriend who helped in our nursery, and felt like God was speaking to him through the worship. He keeps coming to our church, and made a decision to become baptized. I want to create safe places for people like Jay to experience the presence of God in their lives, and receive the chance for healing prayer. In postmodernity the question is not simply, "Is it true?" but "Does it work?" People are testing for an experience of truth. I think a great deal about Paul's words that "our gospel came not only in words, but in a demonstration of the Spirit's power..." I believe that the manifestation of the Spirit's presence will be central in the future church.

One of the miracles people must see in the church is the reality of grace: grace offered to others. I can't believe how "messy" church planting ministry is. I'm always asking what is core and what is contingent in the gospel. I find myself stretched continually. Far more than what I would have guessed, people not connected with the church see the church as being judgmental and legalistic. How do we model something different without selling out our identity? My father, a follower of Jesus who saw the church at various points exercise a huge lack of grace, used to say to me, "Jim, the Bible says judge not." I wrestle with what to hold as core to the gospel, and what to let go, how and when to "speak the truth in love..."

I started this church with no money. The year before we launched I raised my own funds while working part-time at another church. The year we got organized to start, I was in a church planting support group, where most of the others planters were receiving between two hundred to two hundred and fifty thousand dollars from their denominations to start a new church. When they asked me what I was getting, I said "I'm raising my own funds." They said, "Neat." I laughed then, and I've laughed since.

Our denomination came up with support for us the year we launched, but it wasn't a huge dollar amount. There were real disadvantages to this: we couldn't start with part-time staff, and resources were very limited. We had to think through everything carefully. My wife and I were not prepared to do this on a kind of "faith venture" in terms of our family. When we started, our children were twelve, ten and eight.

Modest as it was, I needed a pastor's salary. The advantage of low outside funding, however, was there was not going to be a dramatic cut-off when the funds died. As I prayed, it just felt like God was saying, "focus on the mission of the church, and leave funding issues to me." So I did.

Mostly. Money started to come in. Several business people heard about what we were doing, and approached me about supporting our church. Friends helped support us, and that all added up. God continued to provide. I remember early on when a church (because I had asked them) gave us fourteen hundred and fifty dollars to buy a keyboard for our band. A person who knew about keyboards found one they liked, and the price ended up being four dollars under our budget. I was grateful. I came home after the purchase, so aware of the fact that we needed a keyboard, and also so aware of the money we had just laid out. When I got home, lugging the new keyboard, there was a cheque in the mail from another church that had taken a missions offering for our church. The amount was within a few dollars of what I'd just spent! It felt like another sign that God was with us. Recently we hired a youth pastor part-time. We are not entirely clear where all the money will come from to pay him, but we do have a clear sense this was the right thing to do. Our experience is that when we do God's work God's way, then God will provide.

I knew from the outset that we were called to do this church within our denomination. God honoured the structures that were and were not present in our denomination, and used them to bless us. One of the reasons that our church exists is to model something different in our denomination.

There are numerous leadership issues to face: they are mostly about me. Transitioning from an old established church to a brand new one, my sins walk with me. I'm the same old leader in a new structure. I was trained in a "Christendom" paradigm, where the job of the minister was to do the ministry. I'm trying to equip others to do that ministry now and relearn how I do ministry. Overall, I'm working at becoming more of a team player and being clearer about our vision as a church.

I got tired of the old church structure in the past, but now that I've had a blank slate to work with, my question is different: Is what we are doing any less traditional? I hold the way we do things now very loosely. As Elizabeth O'Connor writes:

> [When] the church starts to be the church it will constantly be adventuring out into places where there are no tried and tested ways. If the church in our day has few prophetic voices to sound above the noises of the street, perhaps in large part it is because the pioneering spirit has become foreign to it. It shows little willingness to explore new ways. Where it does it has often been called an experiment. We would say that the church of Christ is never an experiment, but wherever that church is true to its mission it will be experimenting, pioneering, blazing new paths, seeking how to speak the reconciling Word of God to its own age.
>
> It cannot do this if it is held captive by the structures of another day or is slave to its own structures… (*Call to Commitment*. New York: Harper and Row, 1963) 54.

I have learned that I come with my own unspoken expectations. A close friend says that the reason everyone says yes to my wife, but not to me, when asked to help, is that I have a certain unspoken standard which I expect and which can't be met. When my wife asks people to help, that expectation isn't there; she is simply asking for help. That may be true. I'm working on letting go much more each day, and trusting God to steer the boat.

Part of this letting go is letting Jesus own the church he said was his to begin with. One of the biggest ongoing personal issues for me is always feeling like we have to come up with "the next thing." The weight of the church feels like it rests on me much more than it did with an older church, where history and old momentum carried things much more. In a sense we are blazing a new trail, and it's hard work. I'm always asking the question about what it means to allow God to build this church and what it means for me to open my hands and trust God with the vision in the midst of all our planning.

The other part of my life is keeping my spirit intact. I noticed that when things were rough for the Yorkmen, some were brought down by their difficult circumstances, but others remained hopeful. Preaching, for example, takes much more energy in my current context than it did in my previous one. It feels some Sundays like there is a spiritual pouring out that happens, and it takes me time to recover from that; some Sunday afternoons I can barely function.

Ironically, though it feels like I have more time to focus on my relationship to God, I find that discipline harder, not easier. There is a battle to pioneering ministry that is real, hard to name, but present. My spirit is tested in this undertaking like never before. It seems that God is present to me, and revealing himself to me, yet I don't feel his presence. As I've spent more time praying, and as our church has spent more time praying, it seems God is using us more. Recently, we started a group to pray for our service before it began. The Sunday we began they prayed, "God, bring us at least one family from the community today." That Sunday, several new families from the community showed up.

Paul the apostle prayed, "Pray that God might grant us an open door..." That's my prayer as well: I pray constantly for God to give me an open door into the community. I don't always see the path ahead; I don't know what to do next. I repent regularly for my lack of care for the community we have been called to serve. I struggle as a leader with what it means to have a shepherding gift, yet use it almost all internally to build the church. I'm not a great evangelist; I have a heart for the seeker. I often fight the temptation to just hole up in my office. We have done a reasonable job of connecting with the various cultures within our community through our various acts of service. The administration of the school where we meet tells us that there are about forty different nationalities in the school, but those nationalities are not well represented in our church.

There is much I don't care about as a leader: I don't care if what we are doing makes people into good Mennonites. I care a great deal about whether what we are doing helps form people into followers of Jesus Christ. Labels don't matter much, but the Anabaptist values of service to others, care for the broken, community and discipleship matter to me. I care deeply about the tradition where it calls us to action and engagement with others and serves as a bridge builder.

My heritage of connection with a body that has a record for peace and justice carries well in my conversations with those outside the church. We have this rich heritage of service, but we are less ready to speak about what motivates us. That wasn't the case in our early history, where people died to give voice to their beliefs. I want to retain the best of what we have but also be ready to share the hope God has placed within me.

As a pastor in his mid forties I'm focusing more on the gifts and the call with which God has gifted me, and working less at borrowing models that don't fit my gifts or passions. I'm tired of trying to live like some other leader; by the grace of God I want to become most fully Jim Loepp Thiessen. Most of the leadership models I see serve as spiritual distractions from the work God is calling me to do. I can't wear Saul's armour. I can compare myself to others, then use what I lack as an excuse not to develop my own gifts and abilities.

I'm sold on Alpha, and have used that effectively in our ministry. I believe it works because in our culture we belong before we believe. I want to create as many safe places as possible for belonging. In postmodernity people want an experience of God, and that always seems to happen for people taking the course.

If indeed Jesus has gone ahead of us, then our theological task is something like the Emmaus road: we want others to see how Jesus has been walking with them and they haven't recognized it. In our culture, people are open to the spiritual; we need to come in a complete spirit of non-judgment about their life and experience. As they experience grace from us, they are drawn to the God who loves us unconditionally.

As a church planter, I've walked with messiness beyond my wildest reasoning. If people come to church, and they are not churched, they are often in some kind of life crisis. I try to model deep grace in my interactions with others. When Jesus was engaged with a woman who had five "husbands," he only named that, nothing more. She was freed because he named it, and this got to the centre of her identity. "Come see the man who told me everything I had ever done..." He had spoken to her core need.

I don't try and convert others, rather I let Jesus do that. I've noticed that when people come to know Jesus it has little to do with me. One man recently said to me, "I feel cornered by God..." and he knew that trusting Jesus with his life was his next step of growth.

In the early days we were sometimes quite desperate for more people to help with the work. There were people I wanted to come to help us, but God wasn't calling them to do so. I've learned to trust his call. There have clearly been people whom God has called to join us in this adventure, and they have been God's gift to us. The pressure for workers has lessened now. We have about eighty people in attendance at the time of this writing. God has also protected us from certain people who would have steered us away from the journey he wanted for us. Some Christians too comfortable with safe places would have forced us into calm eddies, and away from the rapids and rocks, where ministry happens. Even more than that, I believe God has a specific calling for our church, and something unique he wants to accomplish through us.

We're still heading towards the bay, paddling hard at points, but overall I'm trying to hoist my sail more, and allow God's Spirit to blow us towards home.

Darryl Dash

Darryl Dash has been a pastor at Richview for almost ten years. He also served as pastor of Park Lawn Baptist Church, a small and colourful church in southwest Toronto, for seven years. Darryl is a graduate of Gordon-Conwell Theological Seminary and writes a column at Christian Week. He lives in Toronto with his wife, Charlene, two children, and a destructive dog. Darryl blogs at www.DashHouse.com.

Richview Baptist Church

– Darryl Dash

I lay awake the night I realized I would be going to Richview Baptist Church, a Fellowship Baptist church in northwest Toronto. I don't know how I knew but I did. It was enough to keep me awake for hours praying that it wouldn't happen.

It was still weeks until I spoke for the first time at Richview. It was months until I made it into the pile of candidates. It was even more months until my name made it to the top of the pile, and then an even longer time until I began as pastor. But for some reason, I sensed that night that I would be going to Richview, and I wasn't happy.

Richview Baptist Church was founded in 1959 in what was then a remote part of Toronto. Over the years it had grown to become the largest church in our denomination in west Toronto, with an average attendance of over 400 people. It was a flagship. When I went to seminary in Toronto, it was already past its prime, but it still had a reputation as an affluent and successful church. Rumor had it that the church was rich enough to hire a research assistant for the pastor. The rumor was untrue, but that's the kind of church it was known to be: big productions, a large building, two seniors residences as part of its ministry, and lots of money.

It was a church that had a lot of pride. It did things well. Its facilities were maintained, and it had standards it tried to keep. People expected quality from its concerts and other special events.

I had also heard the rumblings. Some younger families had grown unhappy with things. Many left, some as part of the westward migration toward the suburbs. The church was no longer growing and had even begun to shrink. The pastor of twenty-three years, a towering and sometimes intimidating man, was leaving.

I'm not usually prone to revelations or mystical experiences, but somehow that evening I had a sense that I would be part of the next chapter of this church's history. I wasn't at all confident in my own abilities, or sure that I wanted to pay the price for the transition that would take place.

I was right to be scared. It's been almost ten years, and it's been even harder than I thought. Transformation has taken place, but it's taken longer than I could have imagined. This is the story of the ongoing transformation of Richview. It's equally the story of the ongoing transformation of me.

The Odds

When I arrived at Richview, sixty per cent of the congregation were seniors. Many of them lived at the seniors residence that is attached to the church. They were used to the ministry of a senior pastor who himself had become a senior citizen.

The church had chosen not to become a church of seniors, an option that may have made sense at the time.

Richview also had a group of younger people who longed for greater freedom. It felt a little like Cuba waiting for Castro to die. They imagined that when the senior pastor retired, real change would take place. They wanted freedom, and it had to happen fast.

Anecdotal evidence says that anyone who follows a pastor of twenty-three years is likely going to have a short and miserable tenure. The odds get considerably worse if the new pastor is thirty-one years old, is following a senior citizen, and the congregation is full of seniors. That's not even taking into account the tensions between those who wanted radical change and those who wanted to preserve the past, or the hurts that came from unresolved conflicts and a long period of decline. Things had been held together by a forceful personality, but now he was gone. Almost everything was against me.

That is how I began as pastor of Richview in July, 1998.

Doing Church Better

I began by working on the basics. To be a missional leader in a traditional setting, you have to start by winning respect. That means covering the basics: preaching, visitation, leadership, visiting committees. I tried to build credibility and to build relationships. I threw myself into covering the basics, and things seemed to be going well.

One of the earliest tensions involved a decision made by the music leaders to disband the choir. The choir was struggling, and the leaders felt that the choir wasn't sustainable. It was the right decision, but it wasn't popular. Back then every decision was ultimately blamed on the senior pastor. I still remember descending the stairs to the basement and entering a room full of unhappy choir members who wanted a meeting. I was called names, and we lost a few people. It was tense but I survived.

As often happens with a new pastor, staff changed. Within six months, the youth pastor left. Within another year, so did our director of worship. We hired a pastor of outreach and discipleship. Our choice was risky. We knew the person we had hired would shake things up.

We also began to use Natural Church Development, a tool that claims to measure church health. We simplified some of our structures and pruned our church schedule. I began to teach on what it means to be the church, and what unity amidst diversity could look like.

I didn't abandon theological reflection, but in looking for answers I drifted toward pragmatic solutions. I grabbed every tool I could find. I attended a Willow Creek Leadership Summit in Chicago. A little later I attended a preaching seminar at Saddleback. I thought that the answer to our problems would be found in methods, techniques, and leadership paradigms.

Richview, though, would never be a Willow Creek or a Saddleback. Imported solutions weren't going to do the trick; I just didn't know it yet. The transformation that would need to take place at Richview would have to be at a much deeper level. I was looking for answers but not finding them.

I was also beginning to experience tension. At home, I had two very young children and a wife who was isolated and experiencing some depression after the birth of our second child. At church, some accused me of moving too slowly, while others were furious at me for moving too quickly. I tried to stay upbeat, but the stresses started to accumulate and I was headed for trouble.

The Breaking Point

I hadn't planned to say it. A youth choir was visiting from another church. They were a bit loud, and I could already imagine the criticism I was going to hear when the service was over. When I got up to preach, I heard myself say, "We would like you to get on board. We really would. But if you have decided to resist and oppose what is happening in this church, it would be better for your own spiritual health, and for everyone, for you to find a church that you can support."

Bill Hybels says it; so do other pastors. But when I said it, you could sense the shock. I got congratulations from some. "It's about time," they said. Many were angry. Some wondered what would happen if people listened, and only a handful of people showed up the following week.

The next morning, one of the elderly power-brokers at the church called to share his thoughts with me. I didn't think I was yelling as I responded, but others in the office said I was.

An elderly woman asked to meet with me. When she arrived, she said she didn't want to meet in my office. Near the front doors would be better, she said, because that's where she'd be making her final exit from the church in a few minutes. She corrected me for my many errors, and informed me that the height of church culture was a couple of centuries ago in Europe. This time I only listened; there was nothing to say.

Someone else made tapes of my sermon and distributed them among those she thought would get angry.

After working to establish credibility and heal divisions, I had become impatient and blown it. I was right to challenge what was happening, but everything was wrong about the way that I did it. I had reached the first of a few breaking points.

The next Sunday, most people did show up. Some left, but many stayed. It looked like I would survive a little longer.

Ongoing Tensions

We lived with ongoing tensions for some time. I remember looking for kind eyes as I preached among those who had their arms crossed.

We continued to try to cultivate variety in our music, offending everyone equally. We lost people, but new people also came, including some seniors. Some newcomers became followers of Christ.

We were no longer a church full of seniors. We had lots of seniors left, but we had a huge number of children and young parents. Some who led music had long hair and played in bands during the week; Richview was changing.

Around this time we initiated a major visioning exercise called Refocusing, led by a consultant from outside the church. Our idea was to bring the church together to discern the future of Richview. I realized that we were so far apart that coming to a common vision would take the participation of the entire congregation. The process was okay, but not everyone participated, and we ended up with more of a wish-list than a God-given vision. People were rightly cynical about previously announced visions that started loudly but were quickly forgotten or replaced with something newer or better.

I should have known we weren't ready for a common vision after we completed one of the exercises. We compiled a church timeline, with different colours representing the different kinds of events. Pink represented the painful events of the church's life. As I looked at the finished timeline, I was overwhelmed by the pink on the wall – painful events that had taken place both in my time and before. Few of these hurts had been recognized or healed.

One Sunday, we lost one of the most respected men in the congregation. People were invited to come to the front in the service and leave a note on a cross, representing their sin or a burden, before receiving communion. Some said it was the best communion service they have ever attended; others walked out. I looked in the foyer and saw a group who had left the service and were visibly upset.

I met with the older gentleman who was at the core of that group, but he couldn't see past the long hair of the worship leader and some of the externals. It was becoming clear that my dream of peaceful coexistence between the factions of the church wasn't going to materialize. That old, respected member left the church that day. At my induction, he had promised to stick with me no matter what. His departure hurt a lot of people.

We were struggling. Some of the pain came from change that had to take place, but some of it came from mistakes that I and other leaders had made. I hadn't expected it to be easy, but it's one thing to know this and another to experience hardship with no guarantee that things would ever work out.

We were making some progress: some of the cranky people were leaving and we were attracting new people. We saw some come to faith. It was messy, but good things were happening among the bad.

I increasingly began to experience rumblings within myself about some of the directions I was taking. Were we really engaging the issues at a deep enough level? I was about to enter a new phase of ministry. It was more of an internal transition, but it was going to be as disruptive as any external force I had faced up to this time.

The Dying Church

Our local denomination held a yearly conference for pastors. That particular year, a speaker came from California to talk about multi-venue worship. It was the way to deal with different tastes in the target audience, he explained, providing different music for different people. It was all about how to do church in a way that appealed to a wider variety of people. As I listened, it struck me that we were giving good answers to all of the wrong questions.

Around that time I attended another conference on turnaround churches. Over lunch, someone made their pitch to the speaker. "We have Willow Creek. We have Natural Church Development. We need your brand, your seminar in Canada too." It seemed that church was driven by competing options driven by tastes, like one would choose cereal from a supermarket shelf.

I began to sense that many of the answers I was chasing after were surface responses. They promised a lot, but they weren't sound nor deep, and they weren't working. I sensed that many of them weren't even answering the right questions.

During these years the Church has fought for self-preservation as though it were an end in itself, and has thereby lost its chance to speak a word of reconciliation to humanity and to the world at large. So our traditional language must perforce become powerless and remain silent, and our Christianity will be confined to praying and doing right to our human brothers and sisters. Christian thinking, speaking and organizing must be reborn out of this praying and this action...It will be a new language...the language of a new righteousness and truth, which proclaims the peace of God with humankind and the advent of his kingdom. – Dietrich Bonhoeffer, *Letters and Papers from Prison*.

When Jesus called followers, I thought, he asked them to take up a cross and deny themselves. He asked them to die to self-interest and self-preservation. Why were we not applying this to churches? Why were we instead offering more options to appeal to more consumers? Where were churches taking up their cross and dying to themselves? Why were we talking more about self-preservation than about following Jesus, even if it cost us our lives? These questions began to consume my thinking.

One Sunday I preached:

What about this - a church that is willing to die to its own interests and welfare, to pick up its cross, and follow Jesus? What about a church that, if faced with a choice between following Jesus into unknown and dangerous territory, and taking a safe route that would lead to growth and health – what about a church that would willingly take the dangerous route in order to follow Jesus?

What does this all look like? Where does it all lead? I have no idea. I know it involves following Jesus, with no regard to what it costs us.

I did write down a few outcomes of this decision. A dying church is one in which:

Its own growth and health is not as important as its willingness to follow Jesus wherever he goes, whatever it costs.

It is willing to turn its back on everything – its building, programs, staff, everything – in order to follow Jesus.

Institutional advancement is not as important as kingdom advancement. The church is not concerned with its own institutional survival.

Pastors are not CEOs managing/leading people toward a goal, and plans/goals/numbers/budgets are not the main thing. Following Jesus has been the main thing. The pastor becomes somebody who's hopefully helping to set the pace in following Jesus, but is only a co-follower with the rest of the people.

The reaction to my message was mixed. The head of our property committee hated it. Someone else asked, "What was that?" I offered few answers, and I didn't know how to get to what I described. I didn't expect instant transformation. However, I began to see beyond institutional and personal survival and the marketing of techniques to pastors who are desperately looking for answers.

At the same time, I began to wonder if it was possible to lead a traditional church to missional faithfulness. I can't tell you how hard it was to pastor while processing these issues. I had a lot more questions than answers, but I was searching.

The Low Point

The hardest part of my time at Richview was still to come. We had lost those who were extremely traditional. At the same time, we had lost those who were progressive and impatient. That left the middle group. They are wonderful people, but it sometimes felt that we had lost our edges and were left with the mushy middle.

We still had a core group of very good people, but there was no question that we were stalled. We were no longer the church we used to be, but it wasn't yet clear what we were becoming. Nor was it clear what would have to change.

To make things worse, two of my close relationships broke apart. Since arriving at Richview I had looked up to a godly woman. Before I came to Richview I was told I could depend on her, even if everyone else let me down. In all the stresses of church, she modelled character, humility, and consistency. Due to some complicated circumstances that were not about me, she decided to leave. This was a huge blow. Others in her family also left the church too. It wasn't healthy. It was profoundly disappointing.

At exactly the same time, a friend spread some of the issues he had with me to his peer group, which was quite large. I knew we had issues, and I thought we were working through them. I wasn't aware that some of these issues had influenced other relationships so strongly. I'm sure it wasn't intentional. The effects lasted for a year and many left the church. One confronted me at a breakfast in a way that lacked both grace and truth. Everybody meant well, but it was awful.

I always knew that Richview would be tough, but I hadn't expected this. We were being hurt by friends, not detractors. We hadn't made as much progress as I had hoped, and things looked stuck. We had experienced a lot of pain – some of it self-inflicted – but we had nothing to show for it. Things just weren't working.

Transformation

I wouldn't have expected positive change to come so soon after this, but that's exactly what happened. Richview is being transformed in real and significant ways. The transformation we longed for is finally beginning to take shape.

One night at the local supermarket, I mentioned to my wife, Charlene, that I didn't know what to do. She said, "I think you know what to do. You're just not doing it." She suggested that we get a group of people together to pray. Up until that time, we were somewhat isolated in our leadership. This was the first time we were able to get together with others and pray for the transformation we had been longing for. The group was safe, and we could open up freely. This group became life-giving for us.

I also began to talk with trusted friends and leaders about what we had been through. Some of them knew some of what had happened, but we had never been honest about some of the hurts. I tend to take a lot of pain before I let anyone know what I'm going through. This leads to isolation. I've learned to change this, and we've become less alone. We are more part of a community of leaders who, together with us, are heading towards greater wholeness. We've also moved formally to a plurality of leaders. Although I still have a unique role on staff, much more of the leadership is shared among this group of leaders who have been recognized as having what it takes to lead at Richview.

I've also undergone a theological transition. Around our lowest point I heard a sermon by a pastor who had been at his church a long time and had just returned from a sabbatical. He reflected on some of his mistakes as pastor, and promised to follow Paul's example to centre his ministry on Christ and him crucified (1 Corinthians 2:2). This was not some narrow traditionalist. He was a seasoned pastor who had seen the fads come and go, and had come to realize that transformation could only come as congregations centred on gospel. This became an important theme in my life.

I also came under the influence of Timothy Keller, a church planter in New York City. Keller pastors a church that looks traditional, but is known for being missional. He is highly respected among those who are conservative, but is also highly respected by those who are pioneering mission-shaped churches. I began to learn from the church he pastors, even though it would be impossible and unadvisable to copy it. Still, it allowed me to picture what a traditional church could look like that is strongly missional and concerned with both teaching and practice, evangelism and social justice.

His teaching has also influenced me. Keller writes:

> We never "get beyond the gospel" in our Christian life to something more "advanced." The gospel is not the first "step" in a "stairway" of truths, rather, it is more like the "hub" in a "wheel" of truth. The gospel is not just the A-B-C's of Christianity, but it is the A to Z of Christianity. The gospel is not just the minimum required doctrine necessary to enter the kingdom, but the way we make all progress in the kingdom.

We are not justified by the gospel and then sanctified by obedience but the gospel is the way we grow (Gal. 3:1-3) and are renewed (Col 1:6). It is the solution to each problem, the key to each closed door, the power through every barrier (Rom 1:16-17).

It is very common in the church to think as follows: "The gospel is for non-Christians. One needs it to be saved. But once saved, you grow through hard work and obedience." But Colossians 1:6 shows that this is a mistake. Both confession and "hard work" that is not arising from and "in line" with the gospel will not sanctify you—it will strangle you. All our problems come from a failure to apply the gospel. Thus when Paul left the Ephesians he committed them "to the word of his grace, which can build you up" (Acts 20:32).

The main problem, then, in the Christian life is that we have not thought out the deep implication of the gospel; we have not "used" the gospel in all parts of our life. Richard Lovelace says that most people's problems are just a failure to be oriented to the gospel – a failure to grasp and believe it through and through. Luther says (on Gal. 2:14), "The truth of the Gospel is the principle article of all Christian doctrine…Most necessary is it that we know this article well, teach it to others, and beat it into their heads continually." The gospel is not easily comprehended. Paul says that the gospel only does its renewing work in us as we understand it in all its truth. All of us, to some degree live around the truth of the gospel but do not "get" it. So the key to continual and deeper spiritual renewal and revival is the continual rediscovery of the gospel. A stage of renewal is always the discovery of a new implication or application of the gospel – seeing more of its truth. This is true for either an individual or a church.

I've seen what Keller says begin to come true. I changed as I began to focus more on the gospel and less on Richview and its problems. I asked a friend if Richview was changing and he said, "Richview hasn't changed. You have." As I began to change, so did Richview.

Whenever we're trying to change a deeply structured belief system, everything in life is called into question – our relationships with loved ones, children, and colleagues; our relationships with authority and major institutions. One group of senior leaders, reflecting on the changes they've gone through, commented that the higher you are in the organization, the more change is required of you personally. Those who have led their organizations into new ways of organizing often say that the most important change was what occurred in themselves. Nothing would have changed in their organizations if they hadn't changed. – Margaret Wheatley in "Goodbye Command and Control," in Leader to Leader, 1997.

It's like a convergence. Just as everything seemed to go wrong before, everything has started to come together. People who probably needed to leave have left. Others have begun to let go of their baggage from the past. I've changed. We lead in community. We are no longer looking for the perfect program to transform our church. We are looking for transformation in deeper places, and finding it there.

There are still lots of challenges, but they're better challenges. We are no longer fighting over music. We aren't shocked when someone steps to the microphone and confesses that they've been clean from cocaine for a month. We have moved from being completely absorbed in our own struggles to wondering how to join God in what he's already doing in our neighbourhood. People are beginning to live missionally. Former enemies are reconciling, and even the critics seem more loving.

We recently hosted an evening with Alan Roxburgh at Richview. Roxburgh teaches, writes, and consults around missional leadership. Roxburgh said, "God is up to something in ordinary local churches. It's important for me to say that – the God who encounters us in Jesus always turns up in the most God-forsaken places."

It's taken longer than we would have liked, but what Roxburgh describes is happening at Richview. My part began with a sleepless night, but it's continuing today. I like where it's going.

Jamie Howison

Jamie Howison is a priest of the Anglican Church of Canada, and the founding pastor of Saint Benedict's Table in Winnipeg. He has worked in full-time ministry in a variety of contexts for over twenty years, but is just now beginning to realize that his knees are too old to play soccer and his taste in music has made a definitive shift, as is evidenced in his move from a subscription to Rolling Stone to now reading Downbeat. The original vision for Saint Benedict's Table was dreamed up in a conversation with his wife, Catherine Pate, while riding the Long Island Railway on the way back from spending two days doing theology with Robert Farrar Capon.

St. Benedict's Table is online http://stbenedictstable.ca.

God is the Interesting Thing[63]

– Jamie Howison

The invitation to do some focused writing around the shape and nature of our church community is a welcome one, in that it is always a useful and healthy thing for a pastoral leader to take a few steps back from day to day ministry in order to offer some reflection around what it is that we think we are doing. At the same time, I find it a fairly daunting prospect to attempt to convey, from what amounts to a standing start, what it is that we've been about these past five years.

I'm almost inclined to say that if you really want to get a feel for what we're about, what you'll really need to do is to come and join us for a Sunday liturgy. Or perhaps for one of our monthly Saturday evening contemplative services, or maybe a session in our ideaExchange series that we hold in this great little used book store. Then afterward, we could arrange to go for coffee so that I can fill in the blanks, offer you some ideas for reading, and pass along a copy of our CD of the original music that has been written from within the context of the community. Maybe after doing all of those things, what I have written here will actually come close to successfully describing life at Saint Benedict's Table. Wishful thinking, I know, but it does speak to just

---

63 Portions of this chapter appeared in different forms in Come to the Table, published by Saint Benedict's Table, and in vol. 4, num. 19 of the online magazine, Catapult.

how hard it is to convey much of a church community's life with just words on paper.

The other challenge, though, has to do with whether I'm writing this as a "church planter" or as a pastoral leader of a community that is making the move from "traditional to emergent; attractional to missional." Those are the broad categories which Brent and Len suggested in their invitation to contribute to this book, and while I suspect many of the other contributors will find it relatively clear which of the two best describes their situation, in the case of our community that fit is a bit less clear.

Yes, we are a new church plant – which brings a kind of freedom but also a whole series of challenges, the least of which was not financial in our earliest days – but we are also a "mission" of the Anglican Diocese of Rupert's Land, and so live within a very specific ecclesial and liturgical context. This too comes with its particular challenges, but it also brings what must be described as freedom: freedom from having to steadily re-invent the proverbial wheel, but also freedom from the kind of anomie or normlessness that can sometimes hamstring a new or renewing community as it seeks to find its identity.

We stand, for instance, within the 450 year liturgical heritage of the Anglican tradition, which means much more than just a towering stack of dusty prayer books and hymnals. There is a continuous line which connects what we do in our Eucharistic worship with what our forebears have been doing for centuries, a line which takes us right back to the visionary reforming work of Thomas Cranmer, the chief architect of the English Book of Common Prayer. This tradition is much, much more than just a set of liturgical texts which can be implemented (or not) by the local church. It is a heritage which is at once liturgical, spiritual and theological, providing a context within which both the corporate body and the individual believer lives out the faith. Now to be sure, our community's liturgical texts and habits are quite different from what Archbishop Cranmer envisioned in the first prayer book of 1549, but there is a continuity which grounds and anchors us. This continuity stretches back and includes the great tradition of the early church fathers on which the prayer book itself is grounded.

From time to time, someone will ask why it is that we have "placed ourselves within the Anglican structure," almost as if we went shopping for a denomination and decided to pick this one as our home location. The implication, of course, is that if need or circumstance made it prudent we could do a denominational switch. Our reality is actually quite different from this, in that Saint Benedict's Table is a local manifestation of the Body of Christ as that is construed and lived out within an Anglican context. We are, in short, Anglican.

On a practical level, this means that we live our ministry and life within a tradition with certain marks, with a particular identity. When in the late 1800s it had become abundantly clear that the Anglican tradition had expanded far beyond its earlier identity as the Church of England, the 1888 Lambeth Conference of bishops from around the communion approved four points by which it marked itself as a communion:

1. The Holy Scriptures of the Old and New Testaments, as "containing all things necessary for salvation," and as being the rule and ultimate standard of faith.

2. The Apostles' Creed, as the Baptismal Symbol; and the Nicene Creed, as the sufficient statements of the Christian Faith.

3. The two Sacraments ordained by Christ Himself – Baptism and the Supper of the Lord – ministered with unfailing use of Christ's Words of Institution, and of the elements ordained by Him.

4. The Historic Episcopate, locally adapted in the methods of its administration to the varying needs of the nations and peoples called of God into the Unity of His Church.[64]

This, then, is our context. Whatever we might do anew – in whatever ways we might seek to recapitulate the tradition – is always grounded in this foundation.

* * * * *

As I mentioned above, Saint Benedict's Table is designated as a mission of the Diocese of Rupert's Land in the Anglican Church of Canada. While we have had this official canonical status since October 2004, the community began to be birthed in the spring of 2003, when a small group of a dozen or so people began to meet bi-weekly for Sunday evening worship. In part inspired by the so-called "emergent church" movement, this group was gathered around a desire to explore the possibility of forming a worshipping community both rooted in the liturgical and theological resources of Anglicanism and open to new expressions which might flow from that tradition. Borrowing a phrase from Robert Webber, we began to describe ourselves as being "rooted in an ancient-future."[65]

It is notable that right from the start our worship, which uses a simple liturgy adapted from the Canadian Book of Alternative Services, was centred around the table. So much so, in fact, that when in August 2003 we made the decision to move to weekly gatherings on an ongoing basis, the choice of the word "table" in our name was both spontaneous and unanimous. Further, that St. Benedict was chosen as the patron was in part due to the Benedictine emphasis on hospitality, on welcoming each guest as Christ.

---

64 F.L. Cross, ed. *The Oxford Dictionary of the Christian Church, 2nd ed* (Oxford University Press, 1983).
65 Robert Webber, *Ancient-Future Faith* (Grand Rapids, Mich: Baker Books, 1999).

For the first ten months or so of weekly gatherings, we met on Sunday evenings at St. Alban's Church, a small and attractive parish building in an urban residential neighbourhood in Winnipeg. Because at the time I was still serving as the pastor of a combined Anglican and Lutheran church community in a Winnipeg suburb, there was a real sense that our gatherings were really just explorations of a possible future together, rather than a fully realized church plant. In fact, because I was more or less "moonlighting" with Saint Benedict's Table, we didn't advertise ourselves widely or really do much together beyond our Sunday evening liturgies.

Still, by the end of that ten-month period we had a steady congregation of some forty-five people on most Sunday evenings, and a respectable projected offering income of some $45,000 for the coming year. This put us in a position of being able to seriously contemplate seeking some seed money from the diocese, in order that we might formalize our status as a new mission, thus allowing me to move into full time stipendiary ministry. While the diocese did not see itself able to provide such funding, All Saints' Church in downtown Winnipeg stepped in to offer a grant of $20,000 a year for two years, and invited us in to their building rent-free. The understanding was that we would stay on at All Saints for a third year, and that if possible we would at that point begin to share some of the costs of ministry in that space. The move to All Saints was made in June 2004, with the grant funding beginning in January 2005. I moved into full-time ministry on the first Sunday of Advent 2004, just over a month after we received official status as a mission of the diocese.

We have now finished our first three years at All Saints – actually, three and a half if you include the six months we were there prior to the beginning of our grant period – and as we had hoped we were able to pay a monthly rental/shared ministry fee of $1,000 during the third year. We have extended our sharing agreement by an additional three years, and are currently exploring how we might increase our "ownership" in the parish building. To this end, we have been given a good sized meeting and program room for our own use, and have begun to explore ways in which we might profitably share some aspects of ministry with the All Saints congregation. The intention here is not to meld the two communities, as they are quite distinct in terms of congregational culture and general ethos, but rather to find ways in which the two communities might support and uphold each other as we share some of our life together.

Aside from worship, virtually everything else we do is carried on outside the walls of the church, and we believe that is as it should be. There are two book groups that meet over breakfast in local restaurants, a weekly home-based Bible study, a monthly educational event held in a used book store, occasional pub evenings ("Theology by the Glass"), and various other points of connection for the community, yet worship is utterly central to all that we are and all that we do. We have continued our pattern of gathering in the evening on Sundays for Eucharistic worship, and have also added a monthly Saturday evening contemplative liturgy of the Word called "Hear the Silence."

All Saints' Church is of neo-Gothic design, configured with a high altar, chancel and rood-screen, with fixed pews seating 450. Pews have been removed from the front, making possible the use of a nave altar. We use a small carved oak table, placed in front of the chancel stairs, as our altar. The presider sits in the front pew, oriented to the table along with the community. The lessons are read from a lectern placed midway down the aisle, and the sermon is usually preached from the middle of the aisle at the front.

The liturgy follows a fairly conventional flow: 1) the community is gathered; 2) the Word is proclaimed and prayer is offered; 3) communion is shared; and, 4) the community is sent out into the world, rejoicing in the power of the Holy Spirit. We continue to use a somewhat simplified version of the communion rite from the Book of Alternative Services, and our basic liturgical text is reproduced in colour from hand-drawn illuminated originals, which are placed in restaurant menu covers and accompanied by a sheet with the music and variable prayers for the week. These coloured "liturgy cards," which have been drawn for us by a gifted member of the community, vary seasonally.

There is nothing particularly startling about the shape of that worship, yet within the basic structure we seek less conventional ways in which to draw the community into a place of openness to the presence of God. The musicians, for instance, remain seated and off to the side. They do not face the congregation, but rather with the congregation are oriented toward the communion table. Though there are different ensembles of players, there is generally a guitar or two, a bass, sometimes a percussionist and often a pianist. The music tends to be meditative, much in the vein of France's monastic Taize community, though written and played with a little more grit and feel; many of our musicians have roots music backgrounds, and it shows.

On Sundays at 7:00pm, the main church bell is sounded and the music just begins. People put down the coffee they had picked up at the back of the church, and make their way quietly to their places to join in the singing. As the music resolves, a sounding bowl is rung and incense is lit as a sign of our ascending prayer. We've learned to let the stillness linger for as long as the bowl resounds; to not rush, as if the quiet is somehow offensive. This is followed by the formal liturgical greeting, which varies seasonally and which bridges us into another piece of music. Depending on the season, this might be in the vein of the traditional Gloria; celebratory and marked by a powerful sense of alleluia. It might be something like a Wesley hymn, recreated by our musicians to feel more earthy and perhaps more evocative, or an original piece by one of our songwriters. Regardless, the focus is on the gathering of this community, to begin to make us ready to hear the Word and share the cup.

Prayer is offered, using the collect prayer appointed for that particular day, and then readings from Scripture are shared. We do follow the Revised Common Lectionary, but tend to use just the appointed Gospel lesson and one of the other two readings. The reading is unrushed, surrounded by silence, and done from a lectern placed in the middle of the congregation. A sermon of no longer than ten or twelve minutes is preached, and a brief silence and a piece of music follow. Prayer is offered by a member of the community; this prayer is both a response to the Word and a calling of this community to be mindful of the needs and pain of the wider world.

Again, this is unrushed, and silence is meant to be as much a part of the prayer as are the words themselves. An invitation is offered for people to offer silent prayers of personal confession, which may also be followed by a sung corporate confession. After the absolution is pronounced, people are invited to share with each other a gesture of Christ's peace, as God has once again offered a reconciling peace to us. As the community again offers worship in song, the table is set for communion. There is no offering plate passed at our worship,[66] and when the gifts are presented at the table, it is the bread and wine for communion (real bread and real wine, thank you very much!) along with donations of fresh produce for the local soup kitchen, which are all brought up the aisle, usually by children of the community.

After the Eucharistic prayer, the bread is broken with the following accompanying statement: "This is the body of Christ; behold what you are; become what you receive." The invitation to communion is made, and while the musicians lead us in a song or simple contemplative chant, the communion is shared in a series of large circles around the table. Members of the community are involved in administering the cup, including quite young children. Again, this is an unhurried process.

Having shared together in the bread and wine, we move fairly quickly to the end of the formal liturgy. A simple blessing is pronounced, an announcement or two are shared (including an open invitation for people to withdraw to the chapel for continued prayer

---

66 To pass a plate is to look to guests and visitors to bolster the community's budget, which is deeply problematic. Instead, we have a basket for offerings on the table at the back of the church, and our assumption is that those who wish to make a donation will do so.

and stillness, if the prospect of a social time around the coffee table at the back of the church seems a little too abrupt a shift!), and a closing song is sung. Again, the tone of the song is determined by the season of the Christian calendar. At Easter or Pentecost, this will be a decidedly celebratory hymn, while in Lent or Advent it is likely to be something more melancholy and evocative.

That's really it. Occasionally we'll build in something quite different: once a percussion trio playing a full out drum piece on Pentecost as an attempt to express something of the raw power of the Spirit; another year we had a juggler on Trinity Sunday, holding the three balls aloft in an unlikely icon for the triune nature of the One; we have always shared sherry and shortbread off the communion table at the very end of the Christmas Eve liturgy as a very visceral reminder that such Holy Days are in fact feast days. Last year we added "mimosas" (sparkling wine and orange juice) to our Easter Day celebrations, and to the delight of the children I fired the cork from the first bottle right to the back of the church, accompanied by a hearty "Alleluia! Christ is Risen!" But those are the festal exceptions to the rule; usually we let the music and stillness, the icons and incense, the bread and wine, the words and prayers, do their work.

In the space at the back of the church is another table which also shapes who and what we are: the table of refreshment. Each week as worship closes, we invite people to gather at that table of hospitality and to share a bit of life over coffee and food. That the church is anchored by twin tables is not accidental, for what the community does at one must be mirrored in the other.[67] Close to that hospitality

---

67 I am aware that at innovative Church of St. Gregory of Nyssa in San Francisco the refreshments are served from the communion table, which is an even more blatant way of connecting the table of communion to the other tables in our lives. Aside from Christmas Eve, when sherry and shortbread are served from our communion table at the end of the liturgy, we have found it more helpful to think in terms of the ways in which all of the tables at which we gather – including the table at the back of the nave, but also those in the coffee shops, in our homes, and at the local pub – mirror and echo the communion table.

table are the large baskets for the fruit and vegetables which have been brought as donations to the soup kitchen. These four baskets, which are filled to overflowing each week, when brought forward with the bread and wine are placed at the base of the communion table.

Again, this is not an accidental thing, that when the community comes forward to feast at the table we see our symbolic offering in the name of the One who called the poor and the hungry blessed. The community is regularly reminded that we should not imagine that a few baskets of fruit will solve the world's hunger and absolve us from responsibility. The baskets are a sacramental thing – a prophetic act directed at ourselves – that keep reminding us that to dare to feast at this table is to be made deeply, even uncomfortably aware of the abiding hunger of the world.

The cumulative effect of this way of celebrating communion is to emphasize our common life together before God. Though certain people are entrusted with roles of leadership – lectors, intercessors, musicians, communion administrants, and not least of all the presider, who is the sole person vested in worship – all are united in our orientation as a people together before God. The open invitation to share in the bread and wine, quite literally around the table in community, is for many a point of entry – or re-entry for those who may have found themselves distanced or alienated from the church of their upbringing – into this local manifestation of the body of Christ. As the following attestations from members of our community will suggest, there is certainly a personal dimension to this participation, but it is one set very much in a corporate context:

"Gathering the community around the table reminds me that I am not alone and that it truly is God who has invited us to the table of our Lord. Receiving these gifts from members of the community reminds me that we are all called to be servants of God." – T.B.

"The offering of bread and wine one-to-one personalizes the experience, the common cup reinforces the communal aspect, and the offering of the elements by people other than a pastor/elder/deacon reminds of the equality of all in Christ." – A.B.

"The free, open coming together at the communion table in front of the church to celebrate the death, resurrection and presence of Christ in the midst of us at that moment filled me with a deep sense of wonder, peace, joy and oneness with all people. There was no exclusion; neither was there any judgment; no prying into myself by other more mature Christians; no shame felt during confession, no sense of 'you don't belong because you are not the same as, or as good as, or as right as. One requirement only – hunger." – M.D.

Pass the cup around
I can hardly speak a word,
And I am lost;
Pass the bread around
I cannot sustain my self,
The day is growing longer;
Every time I come back to this table
I think…I might believe…

We might believe
We long to feast
We might believe…

"Pass the Cup Around"
©Jenny Moore, 2005

It should be noted that our practice is one of what is called "open table," in which the invitation to communion is extended to all who would feel called. There is no requirement that participants be regular attenders at our gatherings or even that they be baptized; rather the single requirement is that a person feel open to, and hungry for, this way of encountering the living Christ in the midst of his body, the Church. Our invitation to communion, adapted from one used in the Iona Community of Scotland, states our theology clearly:

This is the table, not merely of the church, but of Christ.
It is made ready for those who love him
and for those who want to love him more.
So come, whether you have much faith or little;
whether you have tried to follow,
or are afraid you have failed.
Come, because it is Christ who invites you.
It is his will that those who want to meet him might meet him here.

Further, we are quite clear that the hospitable opening of the communion table is not merely a pastoral default setting, but rather a theologically informed choice. Though there is not the space here to lay out this position in detail, we understand our practice of open table to be embedded in the very ethos of our church community, central to our identity as a local manifestation of the body of Christ.[68]

* * * * *

Sometime in the late 1930s, Evelyn Underhill – a highly respected scholar working in the area of Christian spirituality and mysticism – wrote a letter to the Archbishop of Canterbury of her day, outlining what she saw as being crucial for the regeneration of the spiritual life and integrity of the Church of England. "God is the interesting thing," she wrote, and went on to call for the church to withdraw from any activity in which God had somehow been pushed to the margins. Her message was for the clergy to get out of the helping profession – to stop trying to justify their existence as some sort of sanctified social workers – and for the church to drop any pretense of being a club or some generally helpful community agency. If "God is the interesting thing," then the church is first and foremost to be about the worship of God and the cultivation of a people who desire to be steeped in prayer, meditation and study.

---

68 For a detailed outline of this position, see Come to the Table, a small book published by our community and available through our website: www.stbenedictstable.ca.

The Archbishop's response goes unrecorded. In fact, there is no way to be sure that the letter was actually ever sent. In our church community, however, we have taken Underhill's challenge very seriously. We've been at this coming on five years now, and we're just beginning to discover just how deep those basic building blocks can take us: deep into the mystery of God.

And God is the interesting thing.

Re:Fresh

Mentoring

Church Planters and Urban Missionaries in Canada

Paul Martinson

Paul Martinson is a career missionary trainer and a member of the leadership of Youth With A Mission, Canada. Currently, he is the chair of the YWAM Canada Leadership Team, the Director of the YWAM Western Canada District, and council member of the YWAM North American Leadership Council.

Paul is a graduate of Bethany Missionary Training School with a BTh and ordination as both a missionary and pastor. His post-graduate work was through ACTS Seminary, Langley, B.C. with MMin 1997; MACS 1999.

Paul and Sandra have been married thirty-seven years, and she is a registered clinical counsellor and Therapeutic Coordinator for the Okanagan Metis. They have two adult children who are married, with two grandchildren. When not traveling, Paul blogs occasionally at http://paulmartinson.blogspot.com.

Finding Wisdom and Soul-Friends

– Paul Martinson

My name is Paul Martinson and I am the western Canada Director of Youth with a Mission.

With the most rudimentary of strategies and by dint of much effort by an eclectic mix of people, my wife and I were part of a missionary church plant among urban First Nations people in Thunder Bay, Ontario in the late 1970s on into the 1980s. In hindsight we really planted three successive churches – one on top of the other – since the migrant population ebbed and flowed between the challenges of living in the urban world, and family relationships back at people's home reserve communities.

One of the classic dilemmas for a white missionary in such a setting is knowing how to "work your way out of a job," since the ideal of having a native leader seemed to be an important component to what constituted a successful cross-cultural church plant. I think now I would be much more pragmatic about whether the ethnicity of leaders mattered that much, but at the time this seemed to be relevant. So in that context, my wife and I, along with our family of two kids, took a sabbatical and went to a Youth With A Mission (YWAM) Discipleship Training School.

Our goal was personal refreshment after seven years of ministry and also to test the viability of the native elders governing the church without missionaries being present. Our YWAM experience was both intense and wonderfully restorative. We felt like we finally received both mentorship and discipleship in a concentrated package that fostered a new love for the Lord and a renewed desire to serve him in missions. Whatever motivation we had at the beginning of our missionary ministry had over time leaked out of our lives by the "cares of ministry."

The upshot of this time was personal renewal for us as a couple in missions, and the growth of the native church in our absence. It seemed like a perfect opportunity to leave church planting and move to missions training with the idea of multiplying missionaries. To that end over the past twenty-five years I have been involved in mentoring a wide variety of Christian workers in cross-cultural missionary settings in North America, but also Europe and Asia. The following chapter is really a reflection on what I have learned to be important hard-won life lessons, and what I would see to be critical areas to seek out mentoring by others.

One of the major reasons that it was relatively easy to leave our church planting role was the positive impact the YWAM Discipleship Training School (DTS) had on us, both individually and as a couple. We felt like we had finally witnessed what discipleship might have meant for the early church instead of the haphazard discipleship that we had received. Consequently, our church-planting/missionary model of discipleship was equally haphazard and seemed to be centred around attending meetings.

The DTS model is really based on an intensive boot camp type experience. I think it could be successfully argued that the boot camp/retreat/camp experience is modelled on the older monastic order type of spiritual development often called a sodality. The YWAM staff that "pastored" the students were highly relational, not only teaching content, but using many hands-on experiential learning methods with coaching and mentoring as part of the growth paradigm. In addition, the proximity of living so close to others worked subtly on reducing our autonomy, yet not so far as to seduce us into group-think. For me this really pointed out that for the fifteen years that I had been a Christian my discipleship model was based on what I knew rationally, doctrinally, theologically, and intellectually, but not so much on the "softer" side of change such as spiritual/emotional/ psychological health. Therefore, my basic model for discipleship was to get the right knowledge and everything would be okay.

As important as much of the head side of discipleship is, it is not a sufficient model for transformational change. To engraft transformational change, discipleship seems to work well when it is walked out in community. Gunter Krallman writing in a mission classic, *Mentoring for Mission*, cited that Jesus basic mentoring model was the obvious fact that primarily he was "with his disciples".[69] Therefore, as much as we learn from Jesus through the stories about him and his teaching, the bulk of the Gospels covers a very brief accounts of the actual time Jesus taught his disciples in a 24/7 relationship-based discipleship. With respect to mentoring, a foundational need is to adopt some model of discipleship and to find the relationships that foster personal growth.

Essentially, discipleship is a relational paradigm for character growth, and not something that can be packaged and duplicated strictly as a program. Over the years either through self-teaching, but more dynamically through mentored relationships, the following topics have proven invaluable for my own growth as a disciple (learner):

- Seeking out wisdom, versus learning from the school of hard knocks

- Discovering a more holistic view of repentance

- Seeking out "soul friends"

- Learning to soften self

- Learning from a variety of Christian traditions

- Finding a way to work with social and organizational complexity

- Leading from the grassroots as a tempered radical.

Part of the challenge of any list is to determine the "logic" of the list. The above list would satisfy my own mind better as a picture, thus a pie diagram, rather than a bulleted list. If it were a pie diagram, you could read it in any order and each topic would be seen as a piece of the whole. Viewed more holistically, the pie diagram could be seen as a picture of

---

69   Krallmann, Gunter. *Mentoring for Mission*, Jensco Ltd., Hong Kong: 1992.

what I have learned over the past thirty plus years in ministry. Seeing from the whole (the bigger picture) is a major aspect of seeking after wisdom as a learning style, versus learning through the school of hard knocks which tends to have a more fragmented pattern.

My parents raised me to be independent. I am sure that during the age of Dr. Spock this was deemed to be the wise way to raise children, a way to promote both self-reliance and autonomy. However, for me this resulted in too much self experimentation, too many wrong turns, and too many disastrous consequences. I suppose the inevitable "bottoming out" contributed substantially to my salvation, but it took me too long to acknowledge my pride-filled autonomy as a limiting factor in my life.

Given this background it is wonderful to see how God can meet us in our brokenness and offer his love and forgiveness. While the Bible points the prodigal to salvation and a restored relationship with God, much of the Bible is also wisdom literature, designed to prevent us from becoming "prodigal sons," and learn proactively to modify our inner and outer worlds, living in such a way as to please God. Following the wisdom of God's ways comes through personal study of the Bible as a primary source in partnership with the grace of God's energy present through the Holy Spirit.

In addition, however, this wisdom seems to me to be the most attractive when it is seen in real people who have learned to lay aside their own autonomy, submit to God's Word, but to do so in a winsome, humorous, genuine way, not as ones baptized in pickle juice. I have had dozens of mentors in this discipline, but the ones who stand out have not shirked the hard work of study and reading; they live principled lives, but do so with a relational warmth that includes the Trinity and others. There is a point in the Orthodox liturgy where the priest intones, "Wisdom, let us attend!" This attention to wisdom, a reminder prior to the Gospel reading, is equally relevant in recognizing both the Bible's wisdom, and those that model the way of wisdom in their lives as our mentors.

Out of the wisdom tradition there is a very rich understanding of the Biblical concept of repentance. All too often when repentance is cited today, it means to be sorrowful for our sins, to feel guilty, and ashamed to such a degree that one changes his/her ways. While this is an aspect of what the Bible teaches on the subject of repentance, the term "to repent" has a much broader range of meanings and hence a much more in depth understanding of the dynamics of human growth and change. The Greek word translated "to repent" is *metanoia,* literally meaning "to change one's thinking". Therefore, *metanoia* means to change one's thinking (mind), to change one's intention (will) and to change one's behaviour. In this context, when Jesus started his public ministry he said, "Repent for the kingdom of heaven is at hand!" Actually these were the exact same words John the Baptist used in preparing the way for the Messiah to come. And while this does imply quitting sinning and getting right with God, it also is perhaps much more neutral in its convicting emphasis.

Therefore, "Repent, for the kingdom of heaven is a hand" likely means something closer to "Change your thinking about the future coming of the Messiah, the time is now, not future. The kingdom of God is being ushered in your presence, recognize it! Get ready! It is now!" So by implication, God's kingdom intrudes into his world, but it means I need to respond by changing the way I think.

So how does one do this? More to the point, what does it take, or what is the process where I recognize I am not thinking accurately and how do I change my thinking? Does guilt motivate me to do this? Does shame? Does wisdom? Does experience? This seems to be especially applicable in learning to adapt my thinking to God's ways while living and working with others. The broader my intercultural, interpersonal experience, the more I will likely need to change my rational mind and thinking dynamics. Therefore learning to make one's thinking explicit and to open self up to another's perspective is a first step in broadening out repentance as a lifestyle.

The implication of *metanoia* for theology and Christian practice is staggering. Could theology be more emergent, evolving, innovative and organic? If so, what will it take for me to have this type of learning mindset so that I might enter into the perichoretic dance of the Trinity and learn and grow in relationship to God as Three-in-One?[70] Can I, in my daily relationships, in cross-cultural relationships, in interaction with

---

70   Kruger, C. Baxter. *The Great Dance.* Perichoresis Press, Jackson, MS: 2003.

fellow pilgrims on this journey of faith, actually learn over a whole lifetime? To begin to answer some of these questions I have needed the mentoring influence of soul friend, relationships that soften my self (my flesh, my natural humanity), creative metaphors and images that inspire me, and discovery of some of the rich history I inherit from a variety of traditions, backgrounds, and cultures.

I once had a visit with an Orthodox missionary priest in Alaska, who leapt into our initial conversation with the enthusiastic rhetorical question, "Do you know what the greatest thing about the Orthodox Church is?" Of course I had no clue, so Father Paul answered his own question. "It is confession – the ability to unburden your heart about anything, *anything* that is weighing you down!" I am not a stranger to confession, but for me it is basically a private affair and only very rarely does it involve a neutral witness. For the Orthodox and others in the more liturgical types of churches, confession involves publicly confessing sins to a "confessor." This heart-unburdening involves absolution as well, but what the confessor role shows me as an evangelical is how rare it is to have a relationship with someone where I can unburden my heart about anything.

In the Celtic tradition the *anamchara*, the soul friend, was a spiritual director, a pastor, a friend, a judge: one who loved deeply so as to inform a person being mentored of his blind spots so that spiritual growth did not stagnate at a certain level. Over the years I have realized how vital it is to have this type of relationship in one's life. For me it has involved a variety of people for different seasons fulfilling aspects of this role. It is often implied that leaders have this in their covering structures, but rarely have I found this to be true or satisfactory. At the informal end of a continuum, soul friends involve those conversations that are deeply satisfying and matter to one's soul. On the more formal end the discipline requires finding and making appointments with spiritual directors for a monthly check-up. All of this is important soul care to forestall some of the mind-numbing loneliness – or even self-deception – that can exist in the midst of Christian service (quite a source of tension and ambiguity given the relationship we have with God). The image that most speaks to me is the need for myself to soften and yield before the Lord, so that somehow God by his Spirit works above and beyond my own ability to grow and change. For this I need people who love me enough to speak the truth into my life so that I might become more than I am.

In my own journey I have been surprised by the wide variety of inspiration I have had from sources not part of my own spiritual tradition. Brian McLaren captured this sort of breadth of influence in his book, *A Generous Orthodoxy*.[71] This book is McLaren's tribute to the broad impact that the whole Church in all its divergences has had on his own spiritual development. I too recognize that I am a product of not just a relationship with Jesus, but also the mentorship from a distance of Christians from the Orthodox, Catholic, Lutheran, Anabaptist, Charismatic, Anglican, Evangelical, Faith Missions, Postmodern Missions, and the emerging church movement.

Perhaps at one time I would have feared acknowledging such a mongrel pedigree of influences, but now I urge Christian workers to broaden their horizons by embracing the whole body of Christ, especially finding inspiration from those most different from one's own natural spiritual inclinations. Having a more ecumenical viewpoint definitely comes with boundary-blurring risks. However, sectarian exclusivism seems to be more dangerous both to personal spiritual development and advancing the kingdom in ministry.

To see the kingdom requires thinking and promoting metaphors and methods that speak to our current reality. When Jesus talked about putting new wine in new wine skins this was an ancient metaphor that is being worked out today. Many of the new wineskin experiments do not look like what has worked in the past, but it is these new innovations in ministry – anchored by the core orthodox beliefs of the past – that keep us linked to Jesus and promote creative responses to the influence of the Holy Spirit at work in our world.

Generally, linking ancient church with innovation creates a strong field of ambiguity. The tendency in stress between opposites is to resolve the tension by moving to one pole or the other. Another viewpoint, however,

---

71   McLaren, Brian D. *A Generous Orthodoxy*, Zondervan, Grand Rapids, MI,: 2004.

is that creativity is birthed out of the matrix of opposites (perhaps even multiple opposites) clashing with each other. Therefore there is a need to personally find models of living with such ambiguity, and to become creatively adaptable in ministry. While most mentors are as unsure of the future as everyone else, a companion in the journey is an invaluable aid to foresight.

As important as ambiguity is to personal growth, it is also critical to understand how organizations and ministries are coping with increasing complexity and diversity. One of the numerous tools for understanding complexity is the whole interconnected field of what is termed "learning organizations."[72] These are not only educational facilities, but businesses, ministries, churches, and missions that embrace learning as a key means of adapting to the complexities of change that are awash in our world.

One of the disciplines in this field of learning is systems thinking, which is a means of seeing the interconnections of multiple actions within a unifying whole. At one point I was very close to leaving the ministry I am now involved in, but it was "chancing" upon some of the resources of systems thinking that gave me the hope to continue. This is a field of study that is hard work, but there is so much internal and external complexity in organizations that can paralyze progress, that a framework for understanding the system is essential in offering leadership and opposing inertia.

Linked with organizational understanding is the need to continually re-invent the model of Jesus' leadership often dubbed "servant leadership." It seems to me that servant leadership is most applicable to grassroots activities that are more networked than hierarchically structured; more organic than centrally planned; more pneumatically influenced than command and control-driven. Again from a mentoring perspective, this is a whole new field of expertise that might be called "chaordic" mentoring (from blending chaos and order).[73] This is one area where

---

72   A significant introductory text to learning organizations is *The Fifth Discipline*. Senge, Peter. *The Fifth Discipline*, Doubleday, New York, NY: 2006.

73   Hock, Dee. *Birth of the Chaordic Age*, Berrett-Koehler Publishers, Inc., San Francisco, CA: 1999.

finding mentors "outside the box" to create adaptations of missions and ministry that are new wineskins seems absolutely necessary for having hope for an unfolding future.

Just as I had a paradigm shift in discipleship from programs and meetings to relationships and mentors, it seems it is crucial for those moving into ministry to seek out mentors that can help them navigate. Reggie McNeal writes in *A Work of Heart*:

> Contemporary Christian leaders who have chosen not to withdraw from the cultural arena face white-water rapids. Culture roils and churns in the collision of the old with the new. At the dawn of the third Christian millennium, continuity battles with discontinuity; the emergent dances with what is passing away. Leaders of spiritual enterprises, like many of the adherents of the faith, have oars in both currents. The challenge involves getting as many through the rapids as possible, knowing some will never make it. The success of the mission largely depends on the ability of the leader, the river guide, to know how to "read" the water (79).

The navigation metaphor is adept, since some leadership experts are seeing our current world as a perpetual white water rafting type experience.[74] Therefore managing the rapids is not an occasional activity; rather it is now the current norm. To manage rapids might be too strong a controlling metaphor. Perhaps a fitting exhortation would be "Run the rapids with courage! Stay in the boat! Help each other! Rest when you can! See you at the ocean!"

---

74 O,Reilly, Kellie Wardman, Editor. *Managing the Rapids*, Pegasus Communication Inc., Cambridge, Mass.: 1995.

George Werner

George Werner serves in Mission Canada, a team of leaders who facilitate missional work across Canada though the Pentecostal Assemblies of Canada His passion and conviction for the nation comes from over twenty years of pastoral ministry in Ontario and British Columbia.

George and Eileen currently live in rural Ontario with their young adult children. They are involved in ministry at The Embassy and Elevation in Waterloo, a new thriving community of believers who seek to be salt and light in the midst of Canada's emerging culture. He enjoys running, golf and hockey, and finds great pleasure in music and the arts.

Mentoring Creators of Faith Communities in a New Millennium

– George Werner

"What? You're writing this down?" The question came with equal hints of doubt and surprise.

I was sitting in a local café with a young leader who had just left a large established church to create a new faith community in one of Ontario's booming Golden Horseshoe cities. In his former role, he had demonstrated that he was a natural leader who could gather, inspire and mobilize thousands of young adults. He had attracted the attention, rightfully so, of our national fellowship of churches as one to watch. Now, he was at a fresh, new beginning point in his ministry journey, moved by a vision to create a place where people could find God and his destiny for their lives and their community.

I have to confess that I am not a church planter, nor have I ever planted a church. But I do have a keen interest in the whole enterprise of creating new communities of faith in our nation. I lead a department in our national fellowship's central office where I focus on the missional needs of Canada and seek ways to address them effectively. I like to know the men and women in our nation who are doing significant things for the kingdom of God, understanding both the person and the work they are so committed to. So, we sat in the café chatting, a young inspirational leader and a national leader in his denomination. The conversation was quick and warm with bits of laughter – there was no real agenda for this particular conversation. But we did get serious at points as we focused on the realities of leadership in the ever-changing ministry environment of Canada in the 21st century, and in our particular church family context.

As we got more intense and transparent about the glories, challenges and frustrations of leading, the above question was asked, somewhat incredulously. I was the one who asked it.

I was surprised that my words were being recorded because I had not come to this particular meeting with any purpose other than to get to know this young man better. But in the midst of our interaction, some wisdom had apparently emerged in my statements that he did not want to forget. And, in the midst of his writing, a reality became apparent to me about the nature of our relationship. We were friends, for sure, but there was another factor involved—a mentoring factor.

I have never intentionally set out to create mentoring relationships with leaders like this. In fact, in my first interactions with young leaders who dreamt about forming a new faith community for their peers and communities, there was a degree of threat—admittedly, a large degree of threat. Prior to my current role, I served on a pastoral team of six men and women who were committed to creating a local church where people who were searching for spiritual direction for their lives would be warmly embraced. We were a typical seeker-friendly church driven by a desire to make Jesus known in our average-sized Canadian city. Through the use of media, the freshest music, needs-oriented programs and dynamic communicators, our weekly gathering grew to well over 700 people. We were passionate about serving our city and I felt like I was investing in a kingdom venture that was innovative and effective, and that was appealing to a wide range of people. Our church was a young, dynamic group of people and everyone there was glad to be a part of it. Or, so I thought.

Two of our younger team members began to dream and talk about a new expression of our church that would appeal to their peer group. It would be a venture that they could shape and form according to their callings, aspirations and ideals. This new church would meet off-site, on another day of the week. It would be an alternative to the "traditional" church, one that would extend the reach of the kingdom in our city. And, it would require that we re-align the use of some of the people and resources that I had come to count on through the years. My emotional reactions ranged from personal offence that my efforts would be undermined by the loss of resources, to fear that we were experiencing a mutiny within our leadership team. Nevertheless, we moved forward and a few experiments with alternative services on Saturday nights proved that, indeed, the need existed for a different expression of the kingdom in our city.

The experiment was effective but short-lived as pastoral transitions shifted the focus of the team and eventually, the whole church. I moved into my current role with its national focus and through various reading and educational experiences, I became more aware of the vast need for fresh faith communities if our nation was to be impacted by the gospel. My realization was that the need was not simply for new churches, but for new kinds of churches that would speak life and shed light into the growing deadness and darkness of our nation. With this truth firmly implanted in my heart and mind, I set out to meet as many significant leaders as I could. Hence, my café conversation where the revelation came to me: my years of leadership experience, and my reflection on those experiences, though not gained in the same environments as these young leaders, was valuable to them in their own journeys.

One of the key roles older leaders can play in the lives of younger leaders is that of a fellow traveller on the ministry journey. My wife and I were on a vacation in a coastal region of Italy where the rugged, mountainous shoreline provided breathtaking vistas and excellent hiking. We had planned a day trip where we would hike for the day and then return by night to the village where we were staying. As we set out early that morning, we met some fellow Canadians at the first bend of the trail who advised us to take the train to the end and hike back to the village. They had discovered that there was a long gruelling climb halfway out from the village, and their insight allowed us to enjoy a long, easy descent by reversing the direction of our hike. After hours of challenging hiking in the hot sun, the insight our fellow travellers provided made the hike enjoyable—possibly even survivable!

Creating a church in Canada today can be an exciting journey of discovery. There are few, if any, formulas or prescriptions to follow that will guarantee success in the endeavour. Each new community of faith is unique in its setting and focus. New insight and information is needed on a regular basis in order to travel the creative path that leads to an established new local faith community. No one has all the answers. So, a fellow traveller who is committed to learning and passing on what he has learned is a very real asset along the way. The old dictum that two heads are better than one applies here! When two (or more) commit to collaborative learning, the learning curve rises exponentially. But, the understanding must be that no one person is the expert all the time. Each person must take the posture of learning at some point in the journey as the principles of mission and sound leadership emerge to provide bearings and directions for that particular context.

My confession about church planting is not entirely accurate. Even though I have never planted a church, my family and I have been integrally involved in a newly formed community of faith for the past six years. When I began working in our national offices I needed to find a church that we could belong to and invest in. We met a leader in our tribe who at twenty years old had created a church for students at one of Canada's premier universities. Now, three years after that genesis, he and his wife were leading the formation of another Christian community for recent graduates who were newly married and were forming families.

The first gathering we attended on a Sunday morning, forty-eight people gathered in the student pub where Saturday's empty beer bottles were still stacked in cases by the door. The presence of my family of six increased their numbers by fifteen per cent! Even though my wife and I were probably the oldest people there, we resonated with the youthfulness of the gathering, its raw, still-forming identity and the potential it had to influence our city. Based on our years of practical pastoral experience, we were invited to engage in the leadership processes of this emerging church. We admitted our limited knowledge of the dynamics of leading such a new enterprise but we committed to learning, experimenting and risking with them.

The leadership team discovered that at times we had insight that was immediately applicable. We also recognized those moments when we were being enlightened to new realities of ministry that we had never encountered before. Our own lives were enriched as a result. As we have journeyed together for these past years, we have enjoyed remarkable growth in numbers and increased influence in our community. This is not as a result of any one person's expertise, but because we have collaboratively moved toward a commonly shared vision for the people of our city to whom we feel called.

Mentors also need to be advocates for their friends, especially in a denominational context. As you might suspect, as a leader in our national fellowship, I believe that being connected to a larger body of like-minded people is important. The benefits and advantages that affiliation brings to both the individual and the local assembly are numerous. There is a synergy available that multiplies the influence of the collected leaders and churches. More can be accomplished together than separately, whether the issue is global impact, national influence or personal medical insurance and pension plans. But, experience shows that large organizations can be—well—organizations. With rules and regulations, policies and procedures in place that are designed to protect the body and propagate their stated outcomes, denominational structures can sometimes present less than ideal environments for young creative people driven by their ideals and visions. That is the place where an older leader who has weathered some of those stormy dynamics within the system can help a church planter by offering another perspective and asking for patience. A voice of experience can temper a reaction. At the same time, the older leader may have relationships with other leaders that can make a difference in the system for that church planter. As a wise uncle speaks to a father about a special gift for his son, a timely word between leaders can be a blessing to a young leader.

Relationships are one of the key currencies in ministry. Over the years, I've had the privilege of meeting literally hundreds of influential people across Canada who possess both the interest and ability to help others be more effective in their work. Whether it's a special skill or some unique knowledge or an ability to contribute finances, these people are available to help young leaders develop into their full potential. I find great reward in connecting individuals with some need with those who can fill that need. Like a library that contains the best, most relevant books for mission in our current situation, our relational networks allow one to pull the right resource off the shelf to help a leader where she has need. There are times when I will simply pass a young leader a mobile phone number or an email address with a suggestion he or she make a call, using my name as a reference if they feel it is helpful.

Occasionally, I will make an introduction hoping that it will open a door. Other times, it's simply a favorable word to someone who can help, on behalf of a young leader with some need. To be able to bring a need and resource together for kingdom purposes is a blessing all the way around: for me, for the contributor and for the recipient. However, there is some risk to the venture. A mismatch or a poorly timed referral has the potential to damage credibility; wisdom and discernment is necessary. In the end though, how we handle our relationships is a matter of stewardship. We need to care for them as one of the servants caring for his talents, with a "profit" for the Master in mind.

An appropriate, effective relational connection can provide a young leader with another, perhaps unexpected, benefit: affirmation. Everyone likes the proverbial pat on the back. Mentors need to be cheerleaders. Ministry can be thankless work, and even in its best seasons, it demands more from the leader than the average working role would. It is too common for young leaders to live and work sacrificially for a long time with little perceivable progress, and receive no recognition for their dedicated effort. A word of affirmation, or some gesture of appreciation, or a gift of encouragement might make the difference between continued investment or withdrawal or burnout.

The effort to be a cheerleader does not need to be burdensome. A latte and biscotti shared with a church planter can be as refreshing as a weekend off if the conversation is affirming and optimistic. Good words can bring life to a soul that is crushed under the pressures and demands of ministry. But the words need to be true and sincere. Flattery is as hollow to the hungry soul as cotton candy is to the starving stomach. Sentiments that can be trusted are those that are expressed from credible longstanding relationships. Parents understand this. My seventeen-year-old daughter, Hannah, is one of the most confident people I know. There is not much in life that intimidates her. As a result, adults regularly think that she is much older than she really is. Since she was a newborn, her mother and I have expressed our unwavering belief in her and cheered for her in every aspect of her life. And, she has lived up to our beliefs.

What new level could a church planting leader rise to if he or she had a regular shot of sincere affirmation and appreciation?

Cheerleaders rarely say, "To be more successful, you should..." Rather, that is the role of the critic and the expert. Such a statement assumes that the speaker has special knowledge and insight, and that the listener wants to hear it. I don't want to hear from the experts and critics all the time. However, I do continually want to be more effective. Not knowing how to be effective is often a source of tension. A mentor can ease that tension by acting as a coach for the young leader. Coaches don't assume the posture of the expert who has the answers. Rather they take the position of the curious observer who asks appropriate, insightful questions that draw the best out of the other. Their line of questioning can bring clarity to a leader's confusion, or help refocus the vision when life is blurring it with distractions. Coaching allows a leader to realize again that resident within his life is a deposit of passion, gifting and talent from God himself for the mission.

There are times when a younger leader will ask a specific question of a mentor, seeking insight from his or her long experience. Such questions call for caution. It is a privilege to be accepted into the life journey of another who is called and equipped by God. To approach such a relationship as one who directs the life of another, like a chess master moving pawns and rooks, is to potentially abuse the trust that is building in that relationship. A coaching posture respects the dignity and ability of the other, caring for him as a peer.

I am always surprised that young leaders grant me the privilege of being involved in their lives. But I see the privilege as a trust to be stewarded. When all is said and done, I want to hear those most meaningful of all words, "Well done, faithful servant."

Jared Siebert

Jared Siebert grew up in a traditional evangelical home which formed the foundation of his character. His family's openness to having "strangers" live with them sparked a desire to see his faith provide both practical and spiritual help to the community. Ten years ago he and his wife, Katherine, moved to Kingston to help in planting the "Next Church." Today he works in the Free Methodist Church as the National Director of Church Development. His main responsibility is to build for the future through the planting of new kinds of churches. Jared writes random notes to himself at www.jaredsiebert.com.

New Skills for Mentors

– Jared Siebert

My journey as a church planter and cheerleader for church planters began in 1998; until that point I had never heard of church planting.

In and around 1996-1997, a group of friends in Kingston, Ontario were increasingly concerned that their generation, called "X" back in those days, was no longer listening to the channel the church was broadcasting on. They felt compelled to do something about it. Their first attempt on a new channel was to open a café in the heart of the city. The Pool, as it was affectionately known, attracted two kinds of people: Christian young adults like the hosts, and folks from the inner city. While this sort of ministry is useful in its own right, it was hardly what we were after. Our friends were still outside a community of faith.

The group prayed consistently for a couple of years about what to do. God finally spoke clearly to Al Doseger that they should plant a church. Several prayer meetings later and a few trips to "cutting edge" conferences on the future of the church and minds were made up. The Pool closed its doors and began the work of becoming a church.

I joined the team on the first Sunday of January in 1998 to do my final internship for my theology degree. The Free Methodist Church in Canada had recently closed a church and rented us their building in downtown Kingston. The downtown neighbourhood we were born into consisted of a great variety of human types and our church collected the whole set: Queen's University students, single moms and their hyper-active sons, drunks, university profs, granolas, raging grannies, agoraphobic painters, Johnny Paychecks, Wiccans, and the mentally ill.

Nearly half of our congregation in those days was made up of people that would not consider themselves Christians. We finally had a place to bring some of our friends.

The one page plan we developed prior to starting was mostly scrapped in the light of the realities of our new neighbourhood. Our new "ready, shoot, aim" plan had a few simple goals:

We did not want to develop a parking problem. The neighbourhood around the building was designed during classic mixed-use neighbourhood era urbanism. As a result we had about six spaces in the "parking lot". What killed the church before us was that it became a drive-in church: the church was not made up of people that lived in the neighbourhood. We heeded the warning and chose an opposite approach; we adapted to the neighbourhood instead of hoping the neighbourhood would adapt to us. This lost us some of our suburbanite friends. The spiritual climate in our church began to look like the neighbourhood and its people: rough around the edges. This was attractive to some and repulsive to others.

We wanted to foster questions and questioners. Our congregation became a weird concoction of the injured and the detoxing. We took comfort in questions because answers often mock and belittle suffering; sometimes we fail to do the hard work of listening because our answers are so comfortable. To honour the make-up of the congregation we went out of our way to create an environment where questions flourished and answers took a back seat. Folks used to lighter and more straightforward worship fare found it difficult to join in our sustained lament. It was obvious we needed a new hymnody. The church seemed fresh out of questioning songs so we turned to Radiohead, Joan Osbourne, Macy Grey, Ben Harper, Tom Petty, Sheryl Crowe, U2, Coldplay and Johnny Cash to supply us. Each week I tried to preach a new question and folks from the congregation would interrupt if I didn't ask the right ones.

We wanted to have fun. Despite our dark and heavy Sunday gatherings we were equally committed to just having fun. To avoid becoming consumed we made a concerted effort to not take ourselves too so seriously all the time.

As the years wore on it became apparent that this project had actually taken root in the neighbourhood. The early dark days mellowed out as more and more people connected to Christ. Our questioning became less desperate and certain predictable beats and rhythms began to emerge. One beat was the unending flow of people we called "the scratchers," so named from the sounds made by their pads and pens. They were driving from all over to come and see what we were up to and their stories were all the same: they had felt a need to start a church like ours and had come to ask us how we did it. As "question" people and not answer people we often said, "We don't know." The second steady beat came from an endless parade of Queen's students, about to graduate, that wanted to know if there would be a Next Church in their next town.

And the beat went on.

The beat got louder and we weren't sure what it all meant, so our leadership took some time away to ask God the same questions everyone else was asking us. As it turns out God had been laying down the phat beat, and he meant it to become a song about more kinds of churches. We had no idea at the time what that might look like or what part we could possibly play. So, we kept watch and we waited.

Not long afterward, we were approached by the Free Methodist Church in Canada to host a Church Startup Network. The goal of the network was to provide beginning support to some "local" church plants (ie. The Open Door in Montreal, Ecclesiax in Ottawa, The Third Space in Peterborough, etc). Through helping support these fledgling projects the new song began to take shape. After a few years in this new support role, I found myself considering doing this work on a national level. In January of 2005 I left my church plant and began working to plant new kinds of churches across the country with the Free Methodist Church in Canada.

A Changing Landscape

Since setting out to plant a church in 1998 a lot has changed.

On a personal level the biggest change for me has been the move from being a colleague of church planters to being a leader of church planters.

This move has given me a new perspective on the local scene. I used to think all churches were unique (mine especially).

Having seen many churches in all kinds of contexts I am now beginning to see predictable patterns and similarities among them. With each new emerging church plant and with each new "alternative worship service," a new ecclesiology is being fleshed out. As these new kinds of churches move from books, blogs and conferences right into your neighbourhood, a predictable, though perhaps vague, form is being created.

When I first started these ideas existed, for the most part, only on paper and the language was provisional. When I first began we referred to ourselves as a Generation "X" church. We went so far as to capitalize the "X" in neXt. This plan died when our ideas met the neighbourhood. We resumed normal capitalization policies and tried to emphasize the flexibility in the name (as in "We always want to be onto the next thing instead of flogging a dead horse"). While the term did a lot for Douglas Copeland's book sales, it did little to describe what was going on.

After a few years the term du jour was "postmodern". While helpful in that this gave a general philosophical address, the handle "post-modernity" was still not adequate. In recent years we've started using the term "emerging." This term seemed to have a longer shelf life, but whichever label you use, you only caricature the truth, nature, purpose, and activities of the church

What I am witnessing is how these new expressions are giving body and weight to these terms. What is resulting from the terms taking root in soil are what I like to call, "newish innovations." The forms of church are "newish" in the sense that they are new and different in nature and practice but old in the sense of rooted and practical. The church is creating newish types of leadership, but it's still leadership. There may be more power sharing and the goal may be about facilitation but it's still leadership. Some people follow; some people lead. Newish theologies are still orthodox theologies. The church is still recognizable in all this. As Elizabeth O'Connor writes:

> We are not called primarily to create new structures for the
> church in this age; we are not called primarily to a program of

service, or to dream dreams or have visions. We are called first of all to belong to [worship] .. to belong to Jesus Christ as Lord and Savior, and to keep our lives warmed at the hearth of his life. It is there the fire will be lit which will create new structures and programs of service that will draw others into the circle to dream dreams and have visions. (*Call to Commitment,* 94)

I have also noticed a disturbing and growing sense of uncertainty among Christian leaders. One of my first official capacities in my new job was to attend an EFC meeting. The one question burning in their mind was, "what does this postmodern thing mean and how do we find, send out and support new leaders?" More and more, leaders are sitting up, taking notice, and wondering what is going to happen next. There is a growing willingness to leave the old country behind and meet the new world head on. This attitude was rare not long ago, understandable since most of the conversation back then was mostly critical and not hopeful.

The past ten years have also seen the rise of organizations designed to support and encourage the growth of emerging churches. Organizations like Resonate, which began as a website and email list are now able to undertake projects like Meetups (gatherings of like- minded Christians for conversation), Greenhouses (a national network of church planters), Cultivate (a regular regional gathering of Resonators), and this book (a collection of the thoughts of people that have found a home in Resonate). It's becoming harder and harder to feel alone.

New Challenges

As time moves on church planters are facing all kinds of challenges as they try to embed new work in Canadian soil. Some of these challenges come at us from external societal forces. Some of these challenges come at us from within ourselves and our own culture.

Externally, the demographic phenomenon of the aging baby boomers is beginning to challenge new church planting projects. The deep pockets and energy that built the Christian music industry, Christian bookstore and the megachurches of the '90s are beginning to disappear. With the greying of the boomers, the weight of these institutions may be more than we can carry.

One result is less money available to support church planting; thus if a church plant is working exclusively among the poor or college students (or both), the long term survival of the project is unlikely. Church plants will have to find new ways, independent of the larger institutions, to fund themselves. At present some are looking to bi-vocational leadership or unpaid pastors. Others are foregoing building ownership in favour of rented facilities. Still others are recognizing that a whole generation of folks that grew up outside the church are not acquainted with the discipline of giving. These churches are finding news ways to communicate the old story of Christian generosity.

The siren call of the suburbs with their adequate parking, custom designed modern church facilities, a two-car garage, and green space for all has been at full volume for fifty years. Church after church has abandoned its foothold on the street corners at city centre for life in the outer rim. When our inner cities began to decay our churches found the door to city centre shut behind them. New church plants, with designs on the urban core, are struggling against the current. New church plants will have to contend with and overcome urban crowding, inflated property prices, and unfriendly zoning bylaws if they want to regain the foothold our churches once had in our downtowns.

Finally, we will have to face the challenge of ourselves. Being a movement that started on paper, we will have to be flexible and adaptable as our ideas begin to interact with real live people. Not every thing we thought should come to pass will actually take root. If we insist on our ideal of community over the reality, we will move out of step with the people in our neighbourhoods and lose them.

A second challenge related to self is that Christians trained in the church are much more sensitive to the subtleties of theology and the nuances of our tribal culture than their non-Christian neighbours. I have often seen a church become unhelpfully dogmatic about its "new way" of doing or being the church. Oddly enough this danger is even greater if we are well-funded. Funding can act as insulation from the reality of our mission field. We are in danger when our church is not sustained by the soil it is planted in; we then have less motivation for contextual sensitivity. New church plants must learn to distinguish relevance from novelty and effectiveness from "doing it the cool way."

A New Set of Skills for Mentors

Given the changing context, mentors, cheerleaders and supporters of church planting have had to adopt a new set of skills in their work. What follows here are some of things that I have had to think through in my work with church planters.

From Wilderness to Experimental Farm

It is a common misconception that emerging thought necessitates an anti-institutional or anti-systemic stance. The resulting and wildly popular "organic" vs. "institutional" binary is really unhelpful. Instead I encourage the mentor and church plant to locate themselves somewhere on the following spectrum:

Wilderness	Provincial Park	Organic Farm	Classic Farm	Experimental Farm

From left to right there is an increasing level of structure applied to the organic process.

1. Wilderness

Wilderness is anywhere that nature is left up to her own devices. On the surface this can appear to be totally free from structure. However, if you look deeper you will find all kinds of systems at work (water cycles, species interdependencies, seasonal cycles, carbon cycles, etc...). Changes within the system occur when balance is disturbed. For instance, one species may dominate the eco-system during certain times of day or even certain times of year: if one animal population gets infected with disease, or another faces severe shortage of food, populations suffer.

I have never witnessed a church that operates like the wilderness. That doesn't mean they don't exist. Forming a church by its very nature is quite the opposite of leaving people up to their own devices. Churches are born of intention and mission, consequently intention and mission tend toward a greater degree of structure.

2. Provincial Park

The goal of the provincial park is the preservation and conservation of the natural. Provincial parks are created for two reasons: the first is to protect certain areas of the natural world from human encroachment; the second is to provide people with access to these preserves. In a provincial park, the rule of thumb is to generally let things be but to intervene in some cases. Intervention is called for when some part of the system goes out of balance with the rest or when a species is threatened.

In these kinds of churches there is intention and mission and little else. There is no expectation that human interactions produce kingdom growth, and probably no concern to measure it. It is assumed that if you provide people with a generally safe environment they will naturally do the work of God's kingdom.

3. Organic Farm

The Organic Farm is somewhere in the middle of intentional mission and ministry. There is still a sensitivity to ecology and a desire to produce the goods in as natural a way as possible. Organic farms expect a yield from their crops and employ the use of machines, planning and design to see this happen. Organic farms prefer new techniques and technologies that limit intervention as much as possible.

Organic farm churches attempt to balance engineering and management with natural processes. The underlying assumption is that nature does most of the work but needs input and guidance.

4. Classic Farm

The classic farm is a pragmatic business. Technologies or techniques that produce the highest yields are the ones used. While natural processes are supported and known they are constantly corrected and augmented, and sometimes replaced, by chemicals, machinery, planning, design and testing.

Classic farm churches are pragmatic in their pursuit of kingdom growth. Human interaction is developed and guided to produce the highest results. These churches don't spend a lot of time with philosophical "shoulds" and tend to stay focused on "what works."

5. Experimental Farm

Experimental farms are highly controlled environments where all natural processes are studied in detail then imitated with technology and management. The results discovered on these farms become a knowledge base that is sold to classic farms and there the long term effects of the various improvements are studied.

I have yet to encounter a church that much resembles an experimental farm so this is an "ideal" type. The level of manipulation of means and ends in human interaction is impossible outside of a laboratory, prison or cult. The work of church sociologists and church growth experts tends to look at the church through this mechanistic and rationalistic lens. Their observations are often examined and adopted by classic farm churches to determine the utility of what is discovered.

In my experience most emerging church plants occupy space somewhere between the extremes of provincial parks and classic farms.

As a denominational leader my work places me somewhere between those boundaries as well. I cannot leave things to their own devices, but I am part of an organization too small to carry out its own experimental detailed studies. I allow the patterns, direction, foci, and response to emerge as planters pursue their mission; as a rule I allow things to take their natural course rather than make frequent and constant interventions. I want commitment not compliance, and commitment comes with investment and ownership. I want church planters to love their work and to relate first of all to the God who calls them, and then I want to support them as they pursue God's dream for their neighbourhood. I believe God's work happens best and most effectively in an environment where the natural impulses of church planters guide things.

Re:Fresh

Moving Away From Church Growth Principles

From the early '90s until the turn of the century, concepts like saturation church planting and homogeneous unit planting were quite popular. (Their popularity still hasn't died out entirely.) Saturation Church Planting employs mapping and demographics research to determine the location of the next area for planting. One can imagine giant maps of Canada on which we move churches and pastors around like pieces in a giant game of RISK. Homogenous unit planting insists that we divide the human population in certain demographics and then plant according to the tastes and preferences of the chosen segment of the population. I have found both of these concepts problematic.

I prefer a move to grassroots-initiated church planting. I prefer to let people plant where they have the most natural connections and affinity. This works for several reasons.

First and foremost we want all the passion and commitment to live in the heart of the planter and the church plant. The alternative approach is for the passion to live inside the denominational leadership and committees. To us this seems as unnatural and potentially dangerous as removing all of your vital organs and replacing them with external devices. A top down model of church planting is not healthy, viable or sustainable. When it comes to planting churches we place a high value on the planters' commitment to the dreams God has given them rather than their compliance with our mechanisms.

That of course is not to say that as a leader I don't have dreams for this country. My dream (which also happens to be the mission statement of my denomination) is to see a healthy church within reach of every Canadian and beyond. To see that happen we are developing an environment where a broad diversity of church expressions can find a home. Try as I might, I cannot conceive of more diversity and unique expressions than a group of Canadian church planters can.

Right now, as a largely rural and small town type denomination we need to plant more urban and multicultural churches. We have developed some special funds, conversations, training, expertise and support that will help us foster new forms of plant life. We hope by combining these helpful environments with the passion of all kinds of church planters for all kinds of Canadians that something beautiful will grow.

The reproductive work of church planting is "atmosphered" by myself and our denomination but the sole initiative comes from planters.

Moving Away From Being Expert-Driven

Malcolm Gladwell, in his book *Blink,* describes the interesting research work of Vic Braden on of the world's top tennis coaches. Vic has studied hours and hours of video tape and used advanced digital imaging techniques, all in an effort to understand what makes the great players so great. "Almost every pro in the world says that he uses his wrist to roll the racket over the ball when he hits a forehand," but as Vic Braden has discovered this is just not the case. Through digital video imaging he is able to break each of their movements down into the component parts and discover what their secret is: talent. That's right – they can do what they do because they have a gift. Sounds simple enough.

However, Vic Braden has made a much more interesting discovery about athletes; he has discovered that there is a gap between the truth of what the athlete is doing and the athlete's experience of that truth. Many of these tennis pros, after they retire, take what they "know" about tennis and teach it to others. When they coach their students on how to have a killer forehand they encourage them to use their wrists to roll the racket over the ball. While this gives the student something interesting to try and practice it most likely won't do much to improve their tennis game.

I have noticed this same phenomenon in the world of books and conferences on church planting. The writers and speakers distilled the truth of their own stories into a series of easy to digest principles and tips, ready to convey to an eager audience. The audience is curious to know the secret of how they too can grow their church plant to 5,000 – in six easy steps. Some of the things they hear are true and helpful. Some of the things they hear might be interesting to try and practice but won't do much to help their churches.

The truth of how to plant a church is more complex than a book or seminar may lead you to believe. While these types of resources are often very helpful we need to find other ways to help church planters.

That's why I work at creating church planting networks: creative networks of church planters are more vital to a reproductive "atmosphere" than experts and seminars. The power of a network lies in the fact that over time and through the sharing of stories, planters are able to learn so much more about church leadership than any book or conference could dare boast. Something powerful happens when planters walk side by side: they learn the value of support and friends; they learn the importance of accountability; they learn that sometimes you can do everything right and things can still go wrong. And they become co-labourers: they pray for each other; they care for each other. All of this shapes them into better leaders and forges a movement.

Redefine Success

Finally, in my support role for church planters I have had to work to redefine success in our denomination. A steady diet of church growth literature has seriously affected our view of success. Here is where we start when evaluating whether a church plant is successful or not.

The first question we ask is, "Have you done what you set out to do?" If you planned for a sustainable church community are there signs you're building one? If you planned for a church that reaches out to the surrounding community, are there signs that you do this effectively? If things are not turning out as you planned, what have you learned or adapted from your original idea?

The final question we ask is, "Will you plant again?" A successfully living church community reproduces: this is a Biblical mandate. We are not to become unproductive in our knowledge of Christ. The need in Canada is too great for us to allow churches to be satisfied with just themselves.

Ray Levesque

Ray Levesque ("She-nex-kaw") is Tlingit and Cherokee and serves an indigenous church network, New Gatherings.com, with over 200 gatherings located in the Canada, the U.S., Brazil and Guyana. He focuses on leadership, and integrating the principles of sustainable community and economic development. He edits the Talking Circle Journal, the Red Road Journal, and founded the national native pastoral fellowship called Round Dance, with almost 200 leaders.

Ray has a BA from Northwest University in Biblical Literature and Theology, graduate studies at Perkins School of Theology at Southern Methodist University, an MA in Organizational Development from City University, and a DMin (cand) from Bakke Graduate University in Transformational Leadership and First Nations Studies. He is married to Elizabeth Levesque (MA, Fuller) with three grown children and two grandchildren. He teaches in Portuguese and Spanish, and for fun, is a soloist in a black gospel choir.

Helping Aboriginal Leaders Lead

– Ray Levesque

Allowing Cultural Christianity to Flourish

This chapter is written from the perspective of newly created fellowships that are not attempting to replicate the forms of the North American church. There are plenty of native and First Nations churches that have chosen the European way, although motivated by conformity, not liberty.

Planting churches is a relatively modern innovation in Indian Country. It has been modestly successful over the last 500 years – to speak kindly – yet the church's influence remains marginal in both urban and reserve aboriginal communities. This creates quite a tension for someone who is First Nations but also a Christian leader. In some communities, Christian leaders are accused of being traitors, while others are tolerated and others welcomed. But it is different from the majority community that is rarely forced to reflect upon the intersection of ethnicity, community and Christian faith in their own setting.

As the Good News was passed along to aboriginal communities, each messenger brought different ways with them, although they all claim to represent Creator, and his Son Jesus. Often, we were told or forced to give up our own spiritual worldviews. Then, in order to become true followers of God, each of their ministers required us to "become" something else first, whether Anglican, Roman Catholic, Presbyterian or Pentecostal. When individual natives did become Christians within these different denominations, it had the effect of dividing, not uniting the community.

What these visitors have rarely considered is that they force us into a hard choice – that we cannot choose only to follow Jesus, but we must also select a denomination to follow, forcing us – in turn – to reject the other religions by our exclusive choice. This also means that we must exclude our families and other relations who attend other churches. No longer are we encouraged or allowed to worship together, but we must worship what they call "the one true God" in separate buildings. It sometimes makes you wonder if they all don't believe in separate Gods such as the Baptist God or the Methodist God to the exclusion of all the other "false" gods worshipped in other churches.

They violate our values of community, of tolerance and inclusivity. They misinterpret our openness to listen to their message as automatic acceptance and religious conversion. Our church attendance is also misinterpreted as loyalty to a particular denomination – a loyalty they expect us to use in order to exclude all others. If we are discovered to have attended a ceremony, we are chided for backsliding into our heathen ways. We are shamed for wanting to be with our families in our own comfortable cultural setting.

Although we sincerely participate in the church prayers and songs while we are with them, we walk in the knowledge that there were prayers and songs here before they came, and we continue with them today. Most of us are not prepared to give up our original songs, prayers, dances, ceremonies and values, although some do, out of fear of condemnation from our new Christian family, or worse, being rejected by Jesus himself! Of course, just because a ceremony is traditional doesn't mean that it is automatically good for the community, and there are certain ceremonies or practices that I will not participate in. But the majority of ceremonies are not to be feared. This is a difficult teaching for an exclusive church to hear and accept.

Some of us native believers decided we must follow Jesus without the burden and baggage of denominations. We have instead created our own new gatherings, situated in our own local cultures. While our gatherings are not recognizable as churches to most churched Christians, many in our circles are Jesus followers.

Critical Tools Used to Fix Natives

The dominant church constantly evaluates the less powerful members of the Body with tools such as "critical contextualization" [Hiebert] and the Wesleyan Quadrilateral.

Denominational observers remain nervous over our apparent "lack of historical connection" to the larger church, but offer little assistance towards a model of cultural integration. From their perspective, we are charged with adapting their ways to ours; .and in the event of any conflict, the outsider-imposed religion wins.

Our cultures are filtered through the grid of "critical contextualization" while Western culture is given a free pass. Their role in colonization and genocide comes under no scrutiny at all, while our failure to assimilate is regarded as disobedience to God's design.

Methodist founder, John Wesley, gifted the church with his tool for spiritual evaluation, a four-part rubric or grid – the Wesleyan Quadrilateral – as a filter to examine all Christian faith and practice: Scripture, tradition, reason and experience. For those of us in the aboriginal setting however, we long for a more integrated perspective, which would at least add the considerations of history, community, and ceremony.

New Gatherings: New Wineskins for Redskins

Our work, New Gatherings, is active among native populations in Canada, the U.S., Brazil and Guyana. While we are able to relate to a variety of Christian streams, including Evangelical, Pentecostal, Anglican and Roman Catholic, the locus of our identity is found in Christ, as he is understood and interpreted in the local setting. As we train leaders, we try not to burden them with European theological battles created centuries ago. We feel it is unfair to force non-Western leaders to choose sides in the battles of other cultures and times, although we are free to relate to them what we have learned by observation.

We do not pit Catholic against Protestant; we do not elevate Evangelicalism as the highest form of Christianity; we do not ask our pastors to choose between an infallible Pope or an infallible Bible. Of the various theories of the atonement, we do not ask for statements of faith demanding adherence to penal substitutionary atonement or memorial sacrifice, or covenantal or Christus Victor. We realize that we see through a glass darkly, and that there is truth in each perspective – yet no single viewpoint fully satisfies our lack of understanding. No single viewpoint ever could. Our worldviews are generally much more integrative, so we see value in balancing several elements together instead of choosing a single "correct" answer.

The Relationship Equation

Indigenous pastors and other leaders in our indigenous communities are bound together more by relationships than titles or identification with a particular theological or denominational stream. On the one hand, this returns us to the heritage of the early Church, in which unity was a much higher value. In our current generation of Christianity, not only do we defend ourselves from outsider religions such as Hindu and Islam, but we also fight against whichever branch of the Church we don't belong to. So Baptists fight the Roman Catholics, and the Charismatics fight the Presbyterians, ad nauseum. The only church which can be truly trusted is apparently the church where you are a member.

In our First Nations settings, our leaders tend to avoid denominational labels, although some are even ordained by denominations. As natives, we are trying to avoid this exclusive approach, preferring to look for commonalities instead of differences. Part of the difference in native ministry compared to church-centred ministry, is that we are more relational than program-driven. I have seen attempts to introduce programs such as Nicky Gumbel's Alpha program or Rick Warren's 40 Days of Purpose. Native ministers will often poke fun at the many programs that come and go in the Christian bookstores and eventually make their way onto our reserves and native churches. For those of us in ministry among the community, we are not trying to "build the numbers" and get attendance (and tithing) up by introducing such popular programs. We strive for a stronger community, not just a stronger church.

Money and the Medicine Man

In regards to money and financing, we have a different approach than most churches that are building-based. We do love to meet wherever and whenever we can, but the expensive building with professional pastor is not a model that works well for many of us. In the Eastern portion of Canada and the U.S., which was first settled by Europeans, this model is more prevalent. Over on the west coast however, there are less native churches and more traditional practices that have not been eliminated by the Church.

It is a difficult proposal to ask the community to pay for a pastor when they have always had medicine people (medicine = spiritual power), sweat lodge leaders, and other spiritual people who never charged for their services. In fact, Christian pastors fail both tests of the authentic spiritual leader.

First, true leaders do not ask for money, although they are supported in generosity, but not with a salary and benefits arrangement.

Secondly, authentic spiritual leaders are local, and are not travelling from the outside. The travelling itinerant preacher is the opposite of what native communities expect.

We work with our leaders to help them to conform to the local standards of the community. For those who are already members of a community, the battle for acceptance is half over. For those who are outsiders, it helps them to have relatives in the community, or to have lived there, or nearby, or to be from a nearby band or tribe. In other words, it takes more than a Bible college degree and a wife that plays piano to start an aboriginal church.

The majority of our spiritual leaders are bi-vocational, meaning that they support themselves, and often at a great personal sacrifice. This again, however, is one of the hallmarks of a spiritual leader, not a fancy suit or luxury car. As native leaders however, we don't consider ourselves bi-vocational – we just serve the community in the tradition of other medicine (spiritual) people. The closest comparison of our leaders would be the chaplain, one who ministers freely to all regardless of belief, affiliation or church membership. We do ordain our leaders (in a governmentally-recognized way) so that they are able to get into jails, prisons, hospitals and other places where they might be needed.

Spiritual Formation: Creator, Creation, Community and Commerce

For most First Nations' peoples, spirituality is integrated throughout life, so that hunting or dancing or laughing are all spiritual activities. Spiritual formation outside of native communities is generally an individual choice and individual exercise. For native people, spirituality occurs primarily in the community setting and is not the "private matter" that many non-native Christians practice. So our sphere literally revolves around community, and the activity of movement is "commerce." Commerce is not just about trade. Dictionary.com defines commerce as:

- an interchange of goods or commodities; trade; business

- social relations, esp. the exchange of views, attitudes, etc.

- intellectual or spiritual interchange; communion.

As spiritual leaders, we are called to encourage the life and health of the community, spiritually, socially, economically, and both within and without our own group.

The ancient spiritual disciplines of the Christian Church, as brought to mind by author Richard Foster, are common to most religions, including prayer, fasting, solitude, service, study, singing, and meditation. Indigenous people also include various spiritual disciplines, although there is more emphasis on ceremony: spiritual formation in community. In most settings, our spiritual leaders are part of the community, and therefore participate in ceremony. For natives, the incarnational activity of ceremonial participation is missional, in that we are called to be models of community membership. Outsiders promote programs and activities as missional activities, while for natives, relationship itself is missional.

Spiritual formation in our settings combines old and new. We have always trained and mentored spiritual helpers by having them assist us in serving others, whether in practical works of mercy or in ceremonies where they might have a role as a firekeeper, or to sing at the drum, or to prepare the meal. As well, our helpers participate in discussions and dialogues, both face to face and in online forums. Some will read and others will even take advantage of higher education. Our higher value is for one helper to learn from another in the community setting. To bring in a highly educated stranger who does not know our community really goes against the grain of our cultures, although this has not seemed to have slowed down missionaries and tent preachers at all.

Ceremonies 'R Us

As Christians, it is normal for us to practice the sacraments (sacred ceremonies) that Jesus gifted us with: Communion and baptism.

Baptism may take place in a river, with the new believer being submerged in the Four Directions, accompanied by drum songs on the shore, followed by a giveaway. In another place, smoke from sweetgrass might be the baptizing element.

Communion might be as simple as caixiri (fermented manioc juice) and dried fish, or as complex as an entire feast at long white-tableclothed tables in the early evening, followed by "Midnight Table," at the end of several hours of prayers, songs, and dancing.

Most cultures will also have additional ceremonies that are not part of the historical record of the Church, but are normative to the spiritual life of the community. We consider most of our ceremonies to be a gift from Creator, but we also receive ceremonies as gifts from other tribes. Christianity, if it were to have been properly presented, would have come to tribes with these new ceremonies as gifts to the people. Many are still waiting for this to happen.

As in the non-native church world, not every church is a healthy place. As indigenous followers of Jesus, there are certain spiritual leaders and teachings and ceremonies that we do not participate in, but usually it is very clear that we should not participate. For example, in one place people can go to ask the future and have their questions answered by spirits, but we would not participate in or encourage others to go.

However, we as natives must be allowed to make these decisions for ourselves. Cultural outsiders are not equipped to judge cultures other than their own, so their appeal to "critical contextualization" is often just a form of colonization. For example, if a native person were to describe a "helper spirit" that protects them from evil, the non-native Christian would probably decry such a dependence on spirits as animism or polytheism. But if a Christian were to describe the "guardian angel" to a native, the native would say, "Oh, you're talking about a helper spirit."

We want the Church to remember that the difference between good and evil is not a barely discernible thin line, but rather is described in the Bible as "night and day" or "darkness and light." We hope that observers from the Big Church will allow us the courtesy to interpret the Good News within the context of our own cultures instead of forcing us to conform to their culturally-informed theologies and biases. We hope that the Big Church will realize that the Good News is powerful to enter and transform every culture, and that the gospel does not need the influence of Western European theology and methodologies in order for us to follow Christ in an authentic way.

Our Leadership Principles

Without being part of our communities, you might not get to hear how we teach our principles and values. So what do we teach our leaders?

- They are to serve the whole community without expecting a salary

- They are to build and preserve relationships as their highest calling

- Leadership is shared among several, not delegated to a single, paid professional

- Education is useful and can be helpful, but is not the true source of spirituality

- We must be patient with the Big Church while they figure out how to relate to us – now that we are leaders and not just followers

- It is important to find a good trade or business to be financially independent so as to guarantee the ability to be prophetic and speak the truth to all without pandering to the rich or faithful givers

- We follow Jesus and accept his Good News, but our way of following will be our own unique model and will generally not be recognizable to the Big Church as "normal"

  - We try to get along with other Christian groups whenever possible, but to draw the line when abuse enters the picture (such as aggressive, uninvited evangelism)

  - We cooperate with local native spiritual leaders who are our relatives who also serve Creator by serving the people

  - We have a lot to contribute to other communities and people groups outside our community and we should be willing to share our God-given gifts.

Forging Ahead

Drawing Conclusions and Applications

Frank Emanuel

Frank Emanuel is a Vineyard Pastor in Ottawa. He has served in various pastoral roles since 1991. Frank's love for the Church and theology has led him to doctoral studies at Saint Paul University (Ottawa) where he researches political theology emerging from new evangelical movements. He is married with two wonderfully creative little girls. Frank writes, reflects and blogs at www.freedompastor.blogspot.com.

Treasure in Jars of Clay

– Frank Emanuel

Len was in conversation with Frank one day, when Frank asked about Fresh and Re:Fresh. As they talked it struck Len that Frank's community would be a good one to run through the grid developed by the authors of Treasure in Jars of Clay: Patterns of Missional Faithfulness, *which was the follow on work to the outstanding* Missional Church. Treasure in Jars of Clay, *therefore, is not a "how-to" book, but rather addresses the question, "How would you know a missional church if you saw one?" It also encourages communities of faith that are in transition. What in the life of a church indicates that it is missional? How can communities find the courage to move toward being more outward oriented?*

This second book began by taking the twelve indicators of a missional church that grew out of the first book, and then asking people across North America to nominate congregations that fit the indicators. In the process, the authors discovered that the twelve indicators were not adequate. Secondly, they realized that none of the indicators had to do with leaders, yet authority within the congregation was a key factor in the movement toward becoming missional. Finally, the authors realized that what they had were not indicators, but "patterns." The result was the identification of eight patterns of missional faithfulness. – Ed.

* * * * *

Despite our best intentions of planting a traditional Vineyard church, we have taken to calling Freedom Vineyard the "alternative" Vineyard of Ottawa. Our community has been gathering, in a variety of settings, locations and forms, since the fall of 2001. Our parent church is River City Vineyard in Sarnia, about seven hours away, so even from the beginning we have been pretty much on our own. We met first as a group of believers who were less than satisfied with our experiences in various local congregations. We set out to run a six- month trial; we decided that if we were growing spiritually after this period then we had a good case for planting a new church. After that time we were excited to open the group up and see what would happen.

We planted Freedom at a time when the dust had just settled on a particularly tumultuous chapter of the Vineyard's history. The expectations of renewal culture, after the Toronto Blessing, proved to be difficult for many Vineyard churches. The original Ottawa Vineyard church, which some of us had been part of, had fallen apart in the aftermath of this mixed blessing. In practical terms, gone were the days when calling yourself a Vineyard garnered you an instant congregation.

As a result, we spent a lot of the early days figuring out what was actually working and what was not. All of us felt strongly that Ottawa needed the unique contribution a Vineyard could offer, but we were less prepared for the actual contribution of Freedom Vineyard. As church planters, we took a passion for equipping, stirred in a vibrant love of the encounter of God, and we honestly expected a traditional Vineyard to emerge. However, what emerged is not your traditional Vineyard church. Certainly Freedom has Vineyard values in its heart, but the appearance that emerged is completely different from what any of us had experienced before.

The Journey to Where We Are

We started out with a half dozen people who all had a positive history with the Vineyard. Numbers is always an odd game for us because at any given time you can count on a core of about a dozen folk that you can not scare off (believe me, in some cases we have tried), and at the same time a much larger sphere of influence in our city, both inside and outside of the Christian Church. The Freedom groups that spring up meet primarily in homes and rarely have more than a half dozen core people attached to them. We tend to average about eight people in a liturgical meeting, no matter how many people are currently attached to that group. What is fascinating is that groups spring up and shut down as needed and these groups are almost always new mixtures of people. Pastorally, it has been an exciting challenge learning how to care for the groups that rise up and at the same time how to maintain the network of relationships that represents our real community. We learned the hard way not to push groups into existence; rather, when it seems like a new group is ready to find its way to the surface, we gather the people interested in starting this new group and we simply pray.

After a few years of trying to establish a viable Sunday service we began to realize that we should just focus on what God was actually blessing and not worry about the rest. Sundays have never really worked for our community. Twice we have made very serious attempts at running regular Sunday services, even once renting a nice big auditorium. But, the heart of Freedom is in the relationships that are cultivated through the small groups, so we decided to focus there. Instead of developing another place to do church, we turned our attention to making these home groups serious liturgical settings by paying careful attention to how each unique group of people worships, and adjusting the liturgy (order of worship) to fit the particular needs of that group. Our running joke is that we never celebrate the Eucharist the same way twice; this is not entirely true, but it gives you an idea about where our values rest. Our commitment is to the community of people, not the forms of ministry. This shift gives us incredible freedom in the variety of ways our home groups are able express themselves.

Discovering Mission as a Community

Our evangelical heritage gives us a real passion to see others encounter God. Even early on in planting Freedom we would dream and scheme about ways to connect with our neighbours. Many of us had grown skeptical of the effectiveness of traditional methods of evangelism, particularly the confrontational models. While these models offer a dramatic approach to evangelism, really none of us have seen these methods produce much in the way of lasting fruit. In our experience, when you invest time, love, and energy into the lives of others, then people who experience Christ through this ministry tend to develop an unshakable commitment to living out the same good news that they experienced through our lives. The reality is that this kind of evangelism is costly; it is almost never easy.

Evangelism like this can take years and always has the real possibility of not ending in the way that you hope. But we are convinced that this is more akin to the expressed love of God: God offered Jesus in the hope that we would all embrace the gift of salvation. To describe this missional stance we have employed a slogan: one step closer to the Father. As a community we have thrown ourselves into the messy and wonderful process of helping all the people in our lives see and commit to a better vision of God. We encourage one another to live as Christ in this world, and, as a community we create space for that to happen. To facilitate and model this, our home groups are always encouraged to include some sort of non-liturgical social gathering each month; these gatherings have been a major pat of introducing new folks to our community.

Formation and Discipleship

People who transition into our liturgical settings find that we take the corporate role of promoting spiritual maturity seriously. As a church we actually focus more on formation than conversion. Folks who come out are invited to participate in the service regardless of where they are at in their relationship with God.[75] Despite being unabashedly liturgical, we believe that our community is a safe place for folks to jump in and encounter God.

Formation that happens in these settings includes developing a strong relationship to the Scriptures. We foster this relationship in three ways: by creating a dynamic relationship with the narratives of the Gospels, by emphasizing a teaching grounded in the Scriptures, and by fostering a corporate dialogue in which we participate with the Scriptures. This scriptural formation happens mainly through our liturgical settings which follow two distinct forms. The first form is a traditional Vineyard formula consisting of three crescendos: worship in song, teaching, and praying for each other. The teaching in this form is almost always structured around that day's lectional Gospel reading. The format of

---

75   Our model for evangelism is greatly influenced by George G. Hunter, *The Celtic Way of Evangelism: How Christianity Can Reach the West - Again* (Nashville: Abingdon Press, 2000).

teaching can vary from a discussion to a structured sermon, but the small setting allows even the most structured sermon to become interactive.

The second form our liturgy takes is Eucharistic. This form rarely ever includes a sermon, but it always includes the public reading of Scriptures. To proclaim Scripture aloud has been a novel idea for us; it allows us to simply receive the words as they are.[76] Reading in this way places the words of Scripture into the context of a celebration oriented toward the encounter of God; we encounter Christ through the words as opposed to encountering a teaching. In addition we have borrowed an ancient practice of having baptismal candidates read the entire Gospel of Mark with their sponsor on the night before their baptism. For many, even for sponsors who had been Christians for a number of years already, this is the first time they have read an entire Gospel from beginning to end.

Our commitment to reading the Scriptures allows the Word of God to live and breathe in our midst more so than we had previously experienced through messages that simply hop through the epistles. What continues to amaze us is the Biblical literacy of our adherents; they are not just familiar with verses but they know the story and they are not afraid to point out when a teacher takes a verse out of context. Obviously, this changes the way we approach teaching from the Scriptures. Rarely will you hear a teacher at Freedom building cases for ideas with a collection of disconnected verses. We train and encourage our teachers to stay close to the lectional readings of the day and to wrestle with them for a word that speaks to our group. Lectional readings are great for ensuring that our home groups cover a variety of important subjects every year and connect our liturgy to a rich historical Church calendar.

We have also introduced into the times of discussion an exercise that develops a dialectic relationship with the Scriptures. Real dialogue moves in two directions. Much of our previous experience in the church

---

76   The credit really belongs to Dr. John Gibaut who taught an excellent course on liturgy at St. Paul University. In this course we not only explored the history of Christian liturgy, but looked specifically at how every element in the liturgy opened up the possibility to encounter Christ.

has consisted only of starting with the Scriptures and trying to distill a message. The dialectic exercise works in both directions. We start by discussing our lived experience; we talk about our frustrations and fears, our needs and desires. We drill deep into these issues, asking why and how we can live in a world of stark injustice and intense suffering. Then we take our concerns to the Scriptures, particularly the Gospel reading for that day. We ask what that reading says to our situation and also what that situation says to that reading. Through this type of teaching we learn together how to enter into a dialogue with the Scriptures, trusting that in the Scriptures we encounter the God who meets us in the midst of real life.[77]

When we finally stopped trying to do all the things that were expected of a traditional church, specifically the things that were not working with our community, life actually became simpler. In this new found simplicity we were suddenly able to focus on relationships in a more open and relaxed way. Discipleship became something that happened not through a deliberate program, rather, through being present in each others' lives. From living together we were better able to recognize the real discipleship needs in our community and to tailor special equipping workshops to meet those needs. In fact, some of those workshops have so impacted us that we have delivered them to other congregations.

Taking Risks to be Faithful to the Gospel

Our strong relationship with the Word of God has opened up our social conscience. We realize that far from an escapist triumphalism, the Scriptures reveal the incarnational God who enters into the suffering of humanity in order to be a Word of hope. This hope speaks of the transformation of all that has been ravaged by sin, be that sin relational, societal or even political. Quite a few of us are no longer able to turn a blind eye to the rape of our planet any more than we could suffer the rape of a fellow human being.[78] We are willing to take risks on doing

---

77   This is a practice adapted from Latin American based Christian communities that follow a Liberation Theology.

78   Realizing that John 3:16 (ton kosmon) is about the whole created order is key to the conscientisation of our congregation.

what we believe to be right. We encourage one another to consider the political implications of the gospel.

We also take risks to reach those we see as virtually abandoned by the conservative evangelical church. Our conviction is that it is almost impossible to significantly share Christ with people you are not willing to have as part of your life. For example, at Freedom, a number of us have made a point of being an active presence at the local gaming convention.[79] Over the years we have built strong relationships with various gamers in our city which gives us incredible opportunities to be Christ in their lives. We are not outsiders, but many of us are actually gamers too. What we discovered is that there is a deep longing for companions who are spiritually mature, wise and loving. We refuse to abandon people in need to the world; we have made a point of opening up our lives to meet folks where they are at.

We use our strengths of community building as a way of being a blessing to the world. As a church, we encourage our people to form and join affinity groups based on areas that already interest them. These groups are not an official part of our church, but as a church we pray into the relationships from which these groups spring up. Most of the affinity groups that have emerged among our adherents are built around games and movies. It is important for us to make the distinction that these are not deliberate evangelistic outreaches, but opportunities to build real relationships and find places to show the love of Christ to our friends and neighbours. As we build these relationships, it is important not to be covert about our faith. In these relationships we are always on the look-out for the natural ways to live our faith before these people, many of whom have never encountered non-judgmental Christians who were open about their faith.

Affinity groups not only provide a natural network, they also yield an opportunity to step out in faith. Within these affinity groups it is

---

79   The main reason we focus on the convention is through the encouragement of the Christian Gamer's Guild (http://www.christian-gamers-guild.org/) who make it a point to run a gamer-friendly church service at the major conventions in the United States.

important for us to model a life of faith as a natural part of our lives. By far, one of the most exciting ways this is accomplished is through prayer. We like to jump at opportunities to pray for the needs that arise in all of our spheres of influence. Letting a family know that your whole church is praying for their specific need is always an incredible witness. We focus on expressing God's love as a primary motivation for prayer, but we have also found that God is near to all who pray. God often shows up in the lives of the folks around us, and it is only natural that they turn to the safe people of faith when this happens.

God's Heart for the World

In all of our spheres of influence we find people who are living through the messiness of life. One of the great advantages of practicing what we call long-haul evangelism is that people get to see us, warts and all. They realize that being a Christian is not a great panacea that solves every problem; on the contrary, our lives are filled with just as much trouble as everyone else's (John 16:33). But, seeing how we love and accept each other, even in the midst of some horrible situations, is one of the most powerful witnesses we can offer. Recently one of our adherents was sharing with me how it was this unconditional acceptance that drew him into his own relationship with God. Even more exciting is his desire to have that same loving acceptance for the people in his life.

Love in our community is expressed powerfully through our ability to care for each other in times of financial need. A huge advantage of not having the overhead of a building is the ability to respond freely to needs that arise both inside and outside of our congregation. We have tried to model generosity and it has become contagious. I have personally witnessed amazing and even sacrificial generosity being practiced by our people.

Seeing love expressed in a community that cares deeply for each other draws people from the affinity groups into our official church activities. Most often they will transition to home group games or movie nights. Sometimes they will come out to a concert or a party. And some of those will continue to be drawn into our liturgical settings and eventually into the waters of baptism.

Worship as Witness

I have already mentioned that our home groups are unabashedly liturgical. It is always interesting to see new people come into a home group. We recently had a gentleman show up for our Ash Wednesday celebration; his first comment was "this had better not be Pentecostal." Clearly he had some questionable history with Christians so I simply encouraged him to grab a coffee and enjoy himself. Ash Wednesday is a big celebration for Freedom because we happen to run most of our home groups on Wednesday nights. The format is our Eucharistic service, but with a time of marking wrists with ashes using the declaration, "Turn away from sin and be faithful to the gospel." Whoever is leading also prays a personal blessing over the person who came forward to receive the ashes. It has been a profound part of our church life and a beautiful way to kick off Lent. Well, I could see that this visitor was a bit uncomfortable with the service; perhaps it was the lively singing. So while I was blessing people with ashes his cell phone rang. What had happened was God had answered a prayer and after the call he began to share this with us. What was most touching was that he then came forward, received the ashes, and encountered the love of God in a profound way.

The reason we gravitated towards a more traditional form of liturgy has a lot to do with recognizing a deep longing in the hearts of our community. A number of our congregants have either a Catholic or Anglican background, so when we began exploring what it means to be a Eucharistic community, it was only natural to look at the Roman Catholic liturgy. After a few years of experimentation we have settled on a Roman Eucharistic form which we have adapted to better fit our conservative evangelical convictions.[80] For many people in our church, the Eucharist has become the high point in our corporate worship life.

Dependence on the Holy Spirit

Regardless of what forms of liturgy each home group gravitates towards, prayer is always a non-negotiable. We will not start a home group

---

80   The form is an adaptation of Eucharistic Prayer #3 from the Roman Rite.

without first gathering in prayer. The crescendo of prayer is always a part of every liturgical gathering. As we have mentioned already, prayer is a huge way in which we demonstrate how we care for each other. We encourage everyone to pray during that part of our service. This often can surprise new people who are not used to being invited to participate so fully in church. One summer we had a couple Roman Catholics from Latin America join one of our home groups. After the service they came up to me and informed me that it was the priest who always prayed for the people. I just encouraged them to pray silently if that is what they are more comfortable doing. By the end of that summer I was overjoyed as one of these ladies led us in prayer at a coffee shop where we had gathered. Neither of these ladies expects the priest to do all the praying anymore.

Kingdom of God

The focus on active participation in our home groups is really how we express our theology of the kingdom. Our Vineyard heritage has strong ties to the kingdom theology of George Eldon Ladd.[81] This theology stresses the eschatological tension of the now and not yet of God's kingdom, it is really what sets the Vineyard apart from other Pentecostal denominations. For Jesus the gospel is this good news of the kingdom and whenever Jesus announces the kingdom there is always an invitation to orient our lives to what that kingdom looks like. We see the gospel as an invitation to work with God towards the goals of the kingdom as peace, justice, love, hope, and faith. As a church we model active participation rather than passive observation.

We have also found that hands-on workshops are very effective in creating an anticipation of God's expressed reign. One of our most popular workshops is a focus on the prophetic dimension of faith life. We help one another understand the unique ways in which each of us receives the voice of God. What is important for us is that we all learn how to participate in the prophetic and not simply let others hear on our

---

81   A great primer on Vineyard Kingdom Theology can be found in Derek Morphew, *Breakthrough: Discovering the Kingdom* (Cape Town: Vineyard International Publishing, 1991).

behalf. Because we run several exercises designed to help individuals realize that this is a natural part of the Christian experience, we find that the atmosphere in following home groups is charged with expectation. This type of equipping is the key to our eagerness to turn to prayer. We have seen many powerful examples of the inbreaking presence of God's kingdom. We long to be a people of God's presence in this world.

Missional Authority

Pascal understood that we could only convince the mind, but when we simply live out the gospel and not try to convince anyone, people will be convinced by the witness of our authentic lives and long for that in their own lives.[82] Our strongest evangelism comes from just being who we are. Being a church that is more concerned about building relationships than having a polished worship service has opened up doors for us that we never expected. Despite not being the traditional Vineyard we set out to plant in Ottawa, Freedom has far exceeded our expectations as to how a church can impact lives.

But being this kind of church demands a different set of sensibilities. We have had to throw out the typical measures of success. Playing the numbers game has actually led some local churches to not consider us a real church. For us it has nothing to do with the numbers of people we see worshipping in the home groups. It is about the quality of our ministry to whoever comes into our spheres of influence. If we help our friends move "one step closer to the Father," then we are hugely successful. And I know for a fact that we have helped many gain a better understanding and commitment to God.

Part of the Vineyard heritage is the passion to equip and release. Over the years we have seen some amazing people come out to Freedom for just a season and then take what we have given to them to other churches and cities. We have made it a point to bless the comings and goings of all our people. It is always hard to see people go, but it is more important for us to be faithful to God. When new people show up at Freedom we pour ourselves into them as much as we can for as long as they are with us.

---

82 Blaise Pascal, *Pensées*. Nos. 252, 795.

Forging Ahead

Planting Freedom has demanded that we be flexible and allow things to be born, die, and become something new. Success for us is never maintaining, but it is following the ebbs and flows of life as a community of the Spirit.[83]

Where do we go from here?

Throughout the journey of planting Freedom Vineyard we have had many different small groups come and go. We never know what is going to spring up next. When new small groups come to life they bring whole new groups of people ready to experience our kind of community. Because the journey is so exciting we have decided to not be in a rush. Our mentoring pastor from Sarnia, George Esser, likes to remind us that there are no emergencies in the kingdom of God. So we are taking our time listening to the Spirit and following when and where God's Spirit leads. Who knows what the future has for us, but if it is anything like what we have already seen, then I cannot wait.

---

[83] The structure of this essay owes a huge debt to the eight "Patterns of the Missional Church" found in Lois Y. Barrett, ed., *Treasure in Clay Jars: Patterns in Missional Faithfulness* (Grand Rapids: William B. Eerdmans Publishing Company, 2004), p.12 - 14.

Fresh+re:fresh
Afterword

Alan Roxburgh

Alan Roxburgh serves as the vice president for Allelon Canada. He is the Director of Educational Resources throughout North America and serves as the coordinating team leader for the Mission in Western Culture project. He has over twenty-seven years of experience in church leadership as a pastor of congregations in small towns, urban centres and the suburbs and in denominational leadership. As seminary faculty he was responsible for teaching in the areas of leadership development and domestic missiology.

Alan is ordained in the Baptist Federation of Canada. He and Jane, a school principal in Vancouver, Canada, have been married for thirty-seven years and have three grown children whose occupations vary from lawyer, plumber and theologian. He also maintains The Roxburgh Journal on the Allelon site www.allelon.org.

One of the advantages of travelling to many different places across the globe and being involved with such diverse movements of the Spirit in these places is seeing one's own country in fresh ways. Canada is an amazing experiment in citizenship and nation building. Wherever one travels, Canada is a name that is welcomed with interest and energy. We are a deeply blessed people comprised of citizens from many differing cultures and backgrounds. Our cities and towns increasingly reflect the polyglot shape of this vast country from coast to coast to coast.

For someone born after the Second World War and an emigrant to this country, the changes that have re-shaped Canada over the past forty years are immense. They have radically transformed the nature not just of Canada, but what it means to be the church. It doesn't seem very long ago when this country could still be defined as a land of workers shaped by the immensity of the landscape, the richness of its natural resources and the less than comfortable relationship of a French and English divide. While the nation was comprised of many more people groups than these, and while its First Nations peoples languished in obscurity, this was the assumed narrative of Canada.

There was a time, not very long ago, when people like Harold Innis, a friend and inspiration for the devoutly Catholic, and Marshal McLuhan shaped the intellectual horizons of this country. The recent biography of Innis, *Marginal Man*, by Alexander John Watson chronicles not just the importance of this brilliant Canadian but shows his roots in Baptist life in a rural Western Ontario. When Innis returned from the trenches of WWI he was a man who could no longer be shaped by the faith in which he was raised. Anyone seeking to understand the shaping of Christian life in Canada in the last century has to understand the dynamics of transformation that occurred in so many like Innis – while Baptist life went on as if the world hadn't been changed by these global wars of terror (birthed in a Christian modernity), the deeper streams of Canada's identity were already being transformed even in those proud English contexts that had shaped much of Canada's ethos to that point in time. The transformation of the church in Canada has its roots in a period long before the introduction of postmodern language at the beginning of this millennium and we will be short-sighted indeed if we try to engage our time without this awareness.

It doesn't seem that long ago that George Grant wrote *Lament for a Nation*, a book that sought to hold back the Americanization of this nation. Only recently, it seems, we were the nation of Cornelius Krieghoff's Quebec winter scenes or Tom Thompson's Ontario Jack Pines or Emily Carr's West Coast fishing villages. The nation seemed to have a mythos and narrative even while it continually sounded tentative and uncertain about that identity.

All that has changed. Today, we are an incredibly diverse people from so many places with divergent values and spiritual narratives. Some of our best literature comes from people like Michael Ondaatje (*The English Patient*), Ann Michaels (*Fugitive Pieces*) and Yann Martel (*Life of Pi*). These books represent something about the Canada we now inhabit that is new; something that at once beguiles and, sometimes, fills people with a feeling of nostalgia for another time when life seemed far less complex and much easier to navigate. What these books represent, in one sense, is a Canada of new immigrants from all over the world. They are books about people who have been torn from their origins and cast upon a sea of change that has few maps and fewer markers. Canada is richer and more vital just as it is more diverse and divergent. It has become a multi-cultural, pluralist society in which varieties of people groups live side by side, sometimes in tension, often in wonder and delight at this amazing journey that has brought all into a space where there is no longer a single dominant narrative shaping its life.

In one respect there is little fear that Canada will become just an adjunct of our southern neighbour. We are not a melting pot. We don't have the heroic founding stories shaped by mythic figures larger than life. There is no manifest destiny or city on a hill. There are peoples from wildly divergent shores discovering that we are all like the English Patient in this new postmodern context, working furtively with fugitive pieces seeking to make sense of who we are in a postmodern world that increasingly makes the idea of nation state anachronistic.

This is the Canada within which a new generation of leaders must seek to shape Christian life in local churches and through the networks of relationships that connect so many of these churches. The denominations, by and large, have struggled to understand this new context. They were shaped by a fundamentally attractionalist and corporatist understanding of the church in 20th century Canada. Their leaders were mostly trained to be wonderful guardians of a tradition when people came to them or joined their particular brand of European-shaped church life. All of that is nearly gone, in terms of having any viability for Christian witness in the new millennium.

What is striking about a good deal of the church in Canada is the way it claims to be different from all things American but is shaped by the functional rationalism and pragmatism that is American. One is still bemused by the ways in which many church programs and Web downloads are imported from across the border. It remains a strange idiom to hear church leaders speak of re-taking Canada for the gospel as if there was a strategy out there that would return this country to the Christian-like culture it was once-upon-a-time in another galaxy, far, far away. I think we all know by now that there is no going back; we are aware that the Christian story is a background vocal somewhere along the narrative of this culture. We are, to use the wonderful image of Heidegger, "in a new clearing." We are in a space where we have never been before. In the words of my friend Colin Greene, we are in something he calls a *metavista space* where multiple narratives collide in the midst of multiple modernities (See his recent book: *Metavista: Bible, Church and Mission in an Age of Imagination*). Or, closer to home, we as Canadians are in what Charles Taylor describes as a world of multiple social imaginaries – a world in which there is no longer a single, or even several, dominant narratives; one in which the former notions of clear propositions of truth gave way to a far less determined and definable sense of reality. The social imaginary is a more elusive set of self-understandings. It's more about assumed practices, and shared common expectations that aren't usually explicitly spoken of, but they give a group their shared life. We no longer live in a world of a few simple narratives or imaginaries but one populated by such narratives that live side by side and often slide into one another.

This is our new context and it is so unlike our neighbours to the south or anything the church has experienced before in North America – although it has become more and more the case in Europe. As Richard Gwynne wrote more than a decade ago, Canada has become one of the first postmodern states in the world. This is the gift of Canada to the world. One of the important questions that the Canadian context raises for the church is: What does it mean to shape Christian life and form Christian communities in this new clearing? This is the question we, as Canadian Christians, have been gifted with by the Spirit. But we can't simply answer it by saying we're not American, then use every new American church strategy that comes down the pipe; nor can we address this question by following after gurus from others parts of the world who presume they are offering us new formulas. We need to ask what the Spirit is saying to us as Canadians.

We want to claim this but rarely practice it. What an awesome moment to be alive as the church in the midst of such a clearing because this is always the kind of place where the Spirit of God is active making all things new. Just as in the Genesis account of creation and John's account of the new creation in the locked upper room (John 21), the Spirit is hovering over the waters of our clearing-like context, longing to bring new things into being. Canada is a gift – it is a space where we have a chance to re-imagine the church in the polyglot land of multiple imaginaries. This is why we can't turn to our southern friends for answers or programs or much else for that matter. We are in a space where the call of God is to risk in experiments that are rooted in this Canadian imagination, not borrowed from leaders in the U.S. or gurus from some other part of the world.

That's why this set of essays is so important. The stories represent young leaders who find themselves in this clearing where there are few answers, embarking on experiments. In one sense there isn't a simple, single theme that connects them all together. They are diverse stories of diverse communities. They still reflect a Canada comprised of a limited part of the population but they are aware of the new reality and trying to find ways to move beyond the boundaries and limits of their heritage to embrace and inhabit this new clearing which is ours. What I appreciate about these essays is that they are simply telling their stories rather than trying to generalize a process and suggest it's the right way for everyone else. If Canada is about anything at all it is about context, about the need to attend to the local.

Clemens Sedmak (*Doing Local Theology: A Guide for Artisans of a New Humanity*) writes about this kind of work in terms of a cook who goes out to discover the local foods, herbs and spices in order to create a wonderful meal out of that which is around us in the local. It is this earthing of the gospel that one finds present in these essays. No one is running around with a big program or telling people that this is the template and pattern that can be used in every town and city across Canada. These are younger leaders mucking about in the soil and ordinariness of the everyday where they live and serve. In the midst of this rather unspectacular way of life they are learning how to be artisans who are creating something wonderful for the kingdom in their backyards.

We need so many more of these stories. I want to resist the temptation of squeezing from them principles and themes that can then be applied across the board in other places. This is too much a part of the older orthodoxies that believe that if one can just name the right principles, then one will create the right plan and work the right program. In this clearing where we find ourselves, we don't have this option. We are all pioneers, there are no experts. What we need right now are more and more stories like the ones in this collection. We need to hold back on conclusions or the need to give names and programs to what we see. We need many more poets of the Spirit in our neighbourhoods: men and women, young and old, sharing with one another the stories of our experiments in this new clearing. Experiments are, by definition, about trying and failing because that's the way we discover a new future as human beings. I would have been greatly blessed by those who could have encouraged my life in the midst of experimenting and failing. I trust we have come to a new place in Canada where we will bless and celebrate these experimenters of the Spirit and poets of the kingdom.